THE INTEGRATED DISASTER RISK MANAGEMENT FUND

SHARING LESSONS AND ACHIEVEMENTS

OCTOBER 2020

Canada

ADB

© 2020 Asian Development Bank
6 ADB Avenue, Mandaluyong City, 1550 Metro Manila, Philippines
Tel +63 2 8632 4444; Fax +63 2 8636 2444
www.adb.org

Some rights reserved. Published in 2020.

ISBN 978-92-9262-440-8 (print); 978-92-9262-441-5 (electronic); 978-92-9262-442-2 (ebook)
Publication Stock No. TCS200300-2
DOI: http://dx.doi.org/10.22617/TCS200300-2

The views expressed in this publication are those of the authors and do not necessarily reflect the views and policies of the Asian Development Bank (ADB) or its Board of Governors or the governments they represent.

ADB does not guarantee the accuracy of the data included in this publication and accepts no responsibility for any consequence of their use. The mention of specific companies or products of manufacturers does not imply that they are endorsed or recommended by ADB in preference to others of a similar nature that are not mentioned.

By making any designation of or reference to a particular territory or geographic area, or by using the term "country" in this document, ADB does not intend to make any judgments as to the legal or other status of any territory or area.

Please contact pubsmarketing@adb.org if you have questions or comments with respect to content, or if you wish to obtain copyright permission for your intended use that does not fall within these terms, or for permission to use the ADB logo.

Corrigenda to ADB publications may be found at http://www.adb.org/publications/corrigenda.

Notes:
In this publication, "$" refers to United States dollars.
ADB recognizes "Vietnam" as Viet Nam.

On the cover: Children crossing a foot bridge in Barangay Katipunan, Pilar, Surigao del Norte, Philippines; and a farmer's family that lives in Kork Roveang, in Kandor Chrum Commune, Ponhea Kraek District, Tbong Khmom Province, Cambodia. (photos by ADB).

CONTENTS

TABLES, FIGURE, BOXES, AND MAP

ACKNOWLEDGMENTS

This report was prepared under the technical assistance project Integrated Disaster Risk Management Fund: Sharing Lessons, Achievements, and Best Practice of the Asian Development Bank (ADB) financed by the Government of Canada through the ADB-administered Integrated Disaster Risk Management Fund.

The report was prepared under the overall supervision of Steven Goldfinch, Disaster Risk Management Specialist, Sustainable Development and Climate Change Department (SDCC), ADB. Grendel J. Saldevar Perez, Senior Operations Assistant, SDCC, and Anna Karmina Ong-Pantig (consultant) provided invaluable overall coordination support in finalizing the document.

Neil Britton (consultant) led the development of the report. The infographics and layout were done by Kookie Trivino and Rommel Marilla. The document benefited significantly from discussions with and comments received from Arghya Sinha Roy, Senior Climate Change Specialist (Climate Change Adaptation), SDCC, ADB, and Renard Teipelke (consultant).

ABBREVIATIONS

AADMER	ASEAN Agreement on Disaster Management and Emergency Response
ADB	Asian Development Bank
ASEAN	Association of Southeast Asian Nations
ASEC	ASEAN Secretariat
CBDRM	community-based disaster risk management
CCA	climate change adaptation
DMC	developing member country
DRF	disaster risk finance/ing
DRM	disaster risk management
DRR	disaster risk reduction
IDRM	integrated disaster risk management
IWRM	integrated water resources management
GMS	Greater Mekong Subregion
Lao PDR	Lao People's Democratic Republic
MFI	microfinance institution
SEA	Southeast Asia
SMEs	small and medium-sized enterprises
TA	technical assistance
UNDP	United Nations Development Programme

EXECUTIVE SUMMARY

Southeast Asia is home to an estimated 36 million people living below the international poverty line, about 5% of the global total. If efforts to achieve the Sustainable Development Goals in this region are to succeed, undertaking disaster risk-informed developments is not a choice, but a necessity. Natural hazards impact large areas throughout the region, leaving an average financial loss of approximately $5 billion a year—a figure that is growing as climate change, population, economic development, and unplanned urbanization increase. In the last 3 decades, disasters triggered by natural hazards resulted in affected population of more than 397 million. It is in this context that the Government of Canada and the Asian Development Bank (ADB) established the Integrated Disaster Risk Management (IDRM) Fund in February 2013. The Fund was created to advance proactive integrated disaster risk management measures on a regional basis within ADB's developing member countries in Southeast Asia, specifically, Cambodia, Indonesia, Lao People's Democratic Republic, Myanmar, the Philippines, Thailand, and Viet Nam. During its operation, the IDRM Fund funded 19 technical assistance projects.

The IDRM Fund provided incentives for leveraging further investments in IDRM by supporting grant components of investment projects, stand-alone grant investment projects, technical assistance, direct charges, and other activities agreed on between the Government of Canada and ADB to support activities in line with ADB's IDRM approach. A specific requirement was for projects to reflect regional solutions that produce cross-border disaster management. Moreover, actions set out in the Association of Southeast Asian Nations (ASEAN) Agreement on Disaster Management and Emergency Response (AADMER) Work Programme and which were common to the priorities of the IDRM Fund were eligible for support. A gender-focused approach to IDRM was another primary consideration for activities to be covered by the IDRM Fund. All projects were screened from a gender lens. Within these parameters, six outputs were identified as funding priority areas:

(i)   enhanced risk identification and analysis;
(ii)   increased investment in disaster risk reduction;
(iii)   improved access to disaster risk finance solutions, including for the poor and poor women;
(iv)   scaling up of community-based and gender-focused approaches;
(v)   increased regional cooperation of IDRM; and
(vi)   enhanced knowledge and tools for IDRM.

The outcome indicators of the IDRM Fund were achieved, including an increased number of IDRM projects in participating countries and the growing availability of various IDRM-related tools to meet demand from stakeholders, especially vulnerable groups and, particularly, women. Advancing gender equity in DRM was achieved, with support provided to implement gender-focused pilots on strengthening community resilience, setting targets to ensure the participation of women in project activities, organizing policy dialogue to raise awareness and gain high-level commitment for advancing the role of women in resilience building, and developing a knowledge product on women-focused investments in climate and disaster resilience. Approximately 25% of the total fund has supported activities with gender equality as its key focus. Supporting disaster risk management-related priorities of ASEAN was achieved. The total direct support provided by the IDRM Fund toward the implementation of the AADMER Work Programme amounted to approximately 11% of the total amount of allocation approved and supported five out of the eight priority areas of the AADMER Work Programme.

The specific format of the IDRM Fund raised some early issues, in particular, (i) the regional (three countries) characteristic of the Fund at times limited its usage within ADB, given its focus on single countries; (ii) the approach ADB adopted to allow civil society organizations and community-based organizations, which typically do not function at a regional level, to apply for the Fund through an umbrella regional technical assistance; (iii) the significant demand from partners to collaborate with ADB under the Fund and the need to manage expectations in view of the limited availability of resources under the Fund; (iv) the need for flexibility to seize time-bound opportunities and meet new demands to strengthen resilience, such as after large-scale disasters; and (v) ADB's efforts to foster partnerships by proactively encouraging joint proposals from regional partners that address critical gaps in ongoing regional programs. These matters were dealt with by minor modifications to the Design and Monitoring Framework and which enhanced the positive contribution the IDRM Fund made, not least of which was because all approved projects were demand-driven.

The geographical diversity of Southeast Asia. The region that is most prone to hazard with its highlands, coastal plains, and water bodies (photo by Asian Development Bank).

I INTRODUCTION

A. Rationale for the Integrated Disaster Risk Management Fund

The Government of Canada and the Asian Development Bank (ADB) established the Integrated Disaster Risk Management (IDRM) Fund in February 2013. The Fund was created to advance proactive IDRM[1] measures on a regional basis within ADB's developing member countries (DMCs) in Southeast Asia (SEA), specifically, Cambodia, Indonesia, Lao People's Democratic Republic, Myanmar, the Philippines, Thailand, and Viet Nam (refer Map next page). During its operation, the IDRM Fund funded 19 technical assistance (TA) projects, some of them linked, including knowledge-sharing activities,[2] plus two projects not covered by this review.[3]

By financing the IDRM Fund, it was the intention of the Government of Canada to support ADB's DMCs to manage their respective natural hazard risks in line with Strategy 2020.[4] Among all the regions in Asia and the Pacific, the SEA region is one of the most hazard-prone, with its wide geographical diversity that includes highlands, floodplains, coastal plains and deltas, large river systems and major water bodies, and seismically active faults and volcanic zones. Drought, earthquakes, fires, floods, and tropical cyclones or typhoons impact large areas throughout the region, leaving a financial loss of $91 billion for the period 2004–2014[5]—a figure that continues to grow as climate change, population, economic development, and unplanned urbanization increase. The effects can be seen in damage to physical assets (housing, roads, water supply and energy, among others) and losses (changes in economic flow) incurred by physical assets. The impacts of disasters, such as loss of livelihoods and damage to assets, are often felt the most by the poor and vulnerable

---

[1] In the context of the Fund, IDRM is understood as an approach that aims to avoid, lessen, or transfer the adverse effects of natural hazards, especially through investments (infrastructure, capacity building, policy and advisory support, knowledge generation and dissemination, formulation of tools, etc.) in disaster risk reduction (DRR), integration of DRR and climate change adaptation, and disaster risk financing.

[2] Knowledge-sharing activities included forums, meetings, publications, videos, and workshops.

[3] These projects comply with the IDRM Fund guidelines but are organizational: (i) a direct charge for a consultation meeting between ASEAN, the Government of Canada, and ADB (IDRMF-DC-01); and (ii) this review (IDRMF-TA-10). The IDRM Fund also supported an ADB loan in Viet Nam by providing printing costs for publications.

[4] ADB. 2008. *Strategy 2020: The Long-Term Strategic Framework of the Asian Development Bank 2008–2020.* Manila, Philippines: Asian Development Bank.

[5] ASEAN. 2016. *ASEAN Vision 2025 on Disaster Management.* Jakarta: Association of Southeast Asian Nations.

Map 1: Southeast Asia

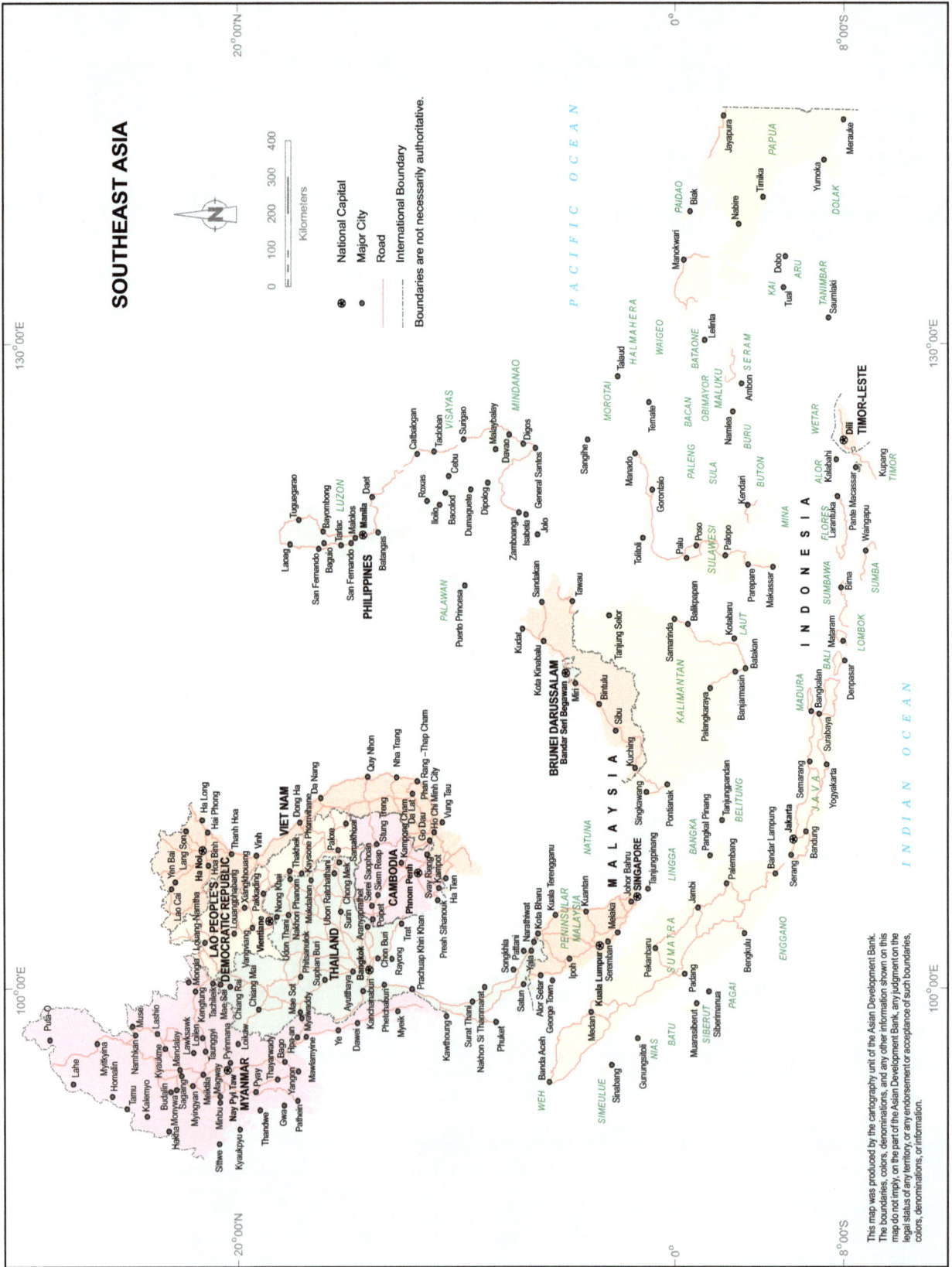

Source: Asian Development Bank.

population with consequences to their long-term well-being. In short, about one in three to four people in the region experienced different types of losses in the period 2004–2014.

In SEA, climate change seems likely to deliver both additional shocks—in the form of greater weather extremes, such as stronger typhoons or cyclones, storm surges, droughts, and floods—and longer-term stresses, such as increasing temperatures and sea level rises, or changes in the availability or location of water (scarcity in some regions, inundation in others). Water scarcity is also population and usage-driven, pointing to the need for integrated water resources management of river basins and underground aquifers to balance water availability and demand.

Managing disaster risk is not only a national concern, but also a transboundary and regional issue. Regional organizations are increasingly active in disaster risk management (DRM), reflecting a trend of growing regional cooperation. A primary vehicle in the SEA region is the work program created by the Association of Southeast Asian Nations (ASEAN), the core function of which is capacity building to help member states improve DRM and develop regional capacity to support preparedness and response capabilities (with a system of rules between member states to expedite collaboration following disaster impacts). A 2015 Declaration on Institutionalising the Resilience of ASEAN and its Communities and Peoples to Disasters and Climate Change addresses risk drivers, such as climate change, uncontrolled urbanization, ecosystem degradation, weak governance, limited risk management capacity, and managing urban and rural development. It underscores the need to align ASEAN's activities to mainstream DRM and climate change and to develop a joint work program for resilience building. However, to be effective, the ASEAN Secretariat (ASEC) needs to build its own capacity.[6]

As with most developing regions, SEA women are at greater risk of economic loss, injury, and death than are men from the consequences of natural hazard impact.

Women and girls face heightened risks because of the social and cultural norms defining gender stereotypes and the breakdown of normal protection structures during crises. Enough evidence has amassed to clearly signal that empowering women can significantly contribute to wider community resilience. Women bring vital skills, knowledge, and experience to building resilience for the straightforward reason that they are holders of intimate frontline knowledge on the local environment, including a good understanding of local-level risk. This awareness is especially useful in identifying and implementing effective resilience-building activities. Natural hazard management programs that promote gender equality and women's empowerment to build climate and disaster resilience will have enduring benefits.

Southeast Asia remains home to an estimated 36 million people living below the international poverty line, about 5% of the global total. If efforts to achieve the Sustainable Development Goals in SEA are to succeed, undertaking disaster risk-informed developments is no longer a choice, but a necessity. Within the IDRM approach established by ADB, four priority action areas are identified to address the region's vulnerability to disasters: (i) institutionalizing disaster risk reduction (DRR) into governance systems and fostering DRM participation among communities, women, and the private sector; (ii) developing disaster risk finance (DRF) options, including the reform of domestic insurance markets and their regulation; (iii) DRM capacity development, particularly with respect to urban disaster risk and addressing the region's vulnerability to water-related disasters; and (iv) addressing challenges, such as linking DRR and climate change adaptation (CCA) actions at both policy and operational levels and enhancing regional DRM coordination. By using an overall IDRM framework that couples disaster risk finance measures with risk reduction and climate adaptation investments, ADB can assist SEA nations to reduce their fiscal exposure to the economic shocks associated with disasters and undertake substantive risk reduction measures to reduce underlying vulnerability. This linkage is central to ADB's IDRM

---

6   Brookings Institution. 2014. *Strengthening Regional and National Capacity for Disaster Risk Management: The Case of ASEAN*. Washington, DC. p. 15.

model and is the main driver in establishing more coordinated and systematic IDRM capability among DMCs. Developing these four priority areas in the SEA region will support the advancement of systematized disaster management policies and programs of individual SEA nations and regional organizations to emphasize DRM approaches and mechanisms, develop finance options to manage the large variances in disaster losses over time, integrate critical constituencies such as communities and women into the DRM process, and develop a total climate risk approach that links disaster risk reduction and CCA.

B. Integrated Disaster Risk Management Fund Priorities

During the two decades of the 21st century, DRM was rapidly evolving conceptually and in practice, globally and within the SEA region (see figure below). At the international level, the United Nations' global blueprint for disaster risk reduction efforts, the Hyogo Framework for Action 2005–2015, which had as its goal the substantial reduction of *disaster losses* in lives and the social, economic, and environmental assets of communities and countries, was succeeded by the Sendai Framework for Disaster Risk Reduction 2015–2030, which emphasized the reduction of *disaster risk* to lives, livelihoods, and health and in the economic, physical, social, cultural, and environmental assets of persons, businesses, communities, and countries. The Sustainable Development Goals, approved in 2015, developed a blueprint to achieve a better and more sustainable future for all by addressing global challenges, including those related to poverty, inequality, climate, environmental degradation, prosperity, and peace and justice. The 2015 Paris Agreement aims to substantially reduce global greenhouse gas emissions to limit global temperature increase to 2 degrees Celsius above preindustrial levels, while pursuing means to limit the increase to 1.5 degrees. At the regional level, ASEAN developed its first ASEAN Agreement on Disaster Management and Emergency Response (AADMER) Work Programme in 2009 and has evolved (the Output 5 chapter explains this further). And at the national level, several countries developed disaster-specific legislation. All

these actions had an influence on the landscape and priorities of the IDRM Fund and, consequently, how it functioned.

As outlined in the overview in Box 1, the IDRM Fund provided incentives for leveraging further investments by SEA nations in IDRM by supporting grant components of investment projects, stand-alone grant investment projects, technical assistance (TA), direct charges, and other activities agreed on between the Government of Canada and ADB to support activities under ADB's IDRM framework. The activities the IDRM Fund drew attention to were intentionally broad to encourage innovative solutions across multiple sectors and professional disciplines. Balancing this was the reality that the IDRM Fund had a limited lifespan, hence projects had to be implemented within that timeframe. The range of activities supported by the Fund were clustered into:

(i)   Disaster risk identification and analysis, including data collection, maintenance and distribution, risk profiling, and mapping and model development.

(ii)   Disaster risk reduction, including land use planning, building code enhancement, infrastructure protection, the strengthening of legal and regulatory frameworks, and disaster contingency planning.

(iii) Disaster risk finance, including insurance sector capacity building, development of public–private partnerships, and disaster risk finance solutions to enhance government disaster liquidity, asset protection schemes, insurance pooling, and increasing insurance access by the poor.

(iv)   Community-based and gender-focused IDRM projects, and other projects aimed at promoting synergies between CCA and disaster risk reduction, including disaster awareness, education modules, needs assessment tools, and early warning systems that address social and gender impacts of natural disasters on the most vulnerable populations.

Increased regional DRM cooperation was important to the IDRM Fund and distinguished it from other funds. A specific requirement was for projects to

Figure 1: Context of Integrated Disaster Risk Management

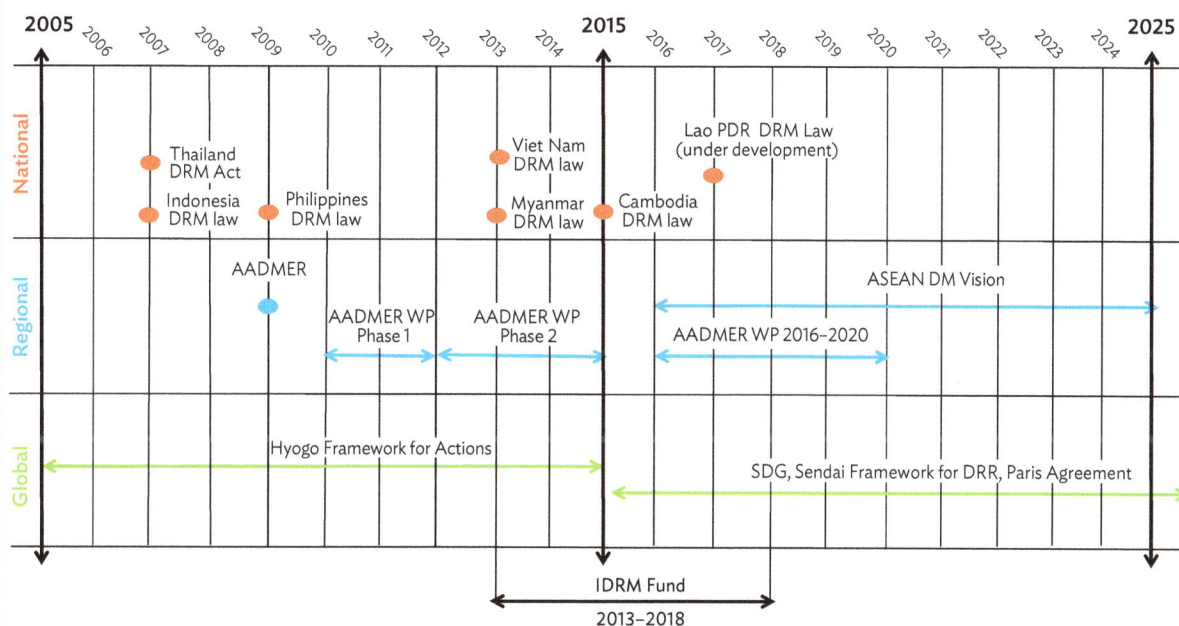

AADMER = ASEAN Agreement on Disaster Management and Emergency Response, DM = Disaster Management, DRM = disaster risk management, DRR = disaster risk reduction, IDRM = integrated disaster risk management, Lao PDR = Lao People's Democratic Republic, SDG = Sustainable Development Goals, WP = Work Programme.

Source: Asian Development Bank.

reflect regional solutions producing cross-border DRM. Moreover, because the Government of Canada's regional development assistance program supported ASEAN, it was appropriate that actions in the ASEAN Agreement on Disaster Management and Emergency Response (AADMER) and which were common to the priorities of the IDRM Fund be eligible for support.

Additionally, and while not a priority output per se, a gender-focused approach to IDRM was a primary consideration for activities to be covered within the IDRM Fund. To ensure projects addressed relevant gender-related issues, proposals were screened from a gender lens and, where relevant, components were made related to the strengthening of women in disaster resilience.

This report reviews the funded projects against these six output areas and discusses the contribution made to these important areas of IDRM engagement. It is important to note that what is highlighted in the review are outcomes that have relevance to outputs as they pertain to SEA nations as a whole and which can be built on in future activities, and not, for example, results that are country- or project-specific. The following matrix (Table 1) illustrates how each project matches up against the six fund outputs. The matrix also reveals those projects which produced knowledge-sharing activities (some generating several, see Appendix 1) and which projects were complemented by meetings, either in the form of workshops or forums. However, before going further, it is helpful to provide an overview of each project.

> ## Box 1: Overview of the Integrated Disaster Risk Management Fund
>
> **Expected Outcome:** Increased access to, and use of, integrated disaster risk management (IDRM) tools in Southeast Asia by key stakeholders, including vulnerable groups, particularly women.
>
> **Priority Outputs:**
> (i)   Enhanced risk identification and analysis
> (ii) Increased investment in disaster risk reduction
> (iii) Improved access to disaster risk finance, including for the poor and, particularly, poor women
> (iv) Scaling up of community-based and gender-focused approaches
> (v)   Increased regional cooperation on integrated disaster risk management
> (vi) Enhanced knowledge and tools for integrated disaster risk management
>
> **Scope:** To meet its regional objectives, the IDRM Fund supports investments that meet one of the following three criteria: (i) have activities in three or more countries; (ii) have certain activities in less than three countries provided the activities not only address issues that are common to the region, but also include other activities in which three or more countries participate and contribute to the results of the entire investment; and (iii) support activities of regional institutions, such as the Association of Southeast Asian Nations.
>
> **Eligible Countries:** ADB's developing member countries in Southeast Asia—Cambodia, Indonesia, Lao People's Democratic Republic, Myanmar, the Philippines, Thailand, and Viet Nam.
>
> **Types of Support:** The IDRM Fund supports grant component of ADB-financed investment projects (loans), stand-alone grant investment projects (grants), technical assistance (TA) projects, and direct charges to fund activities that have not been developed as specific project proposal, but are directly related to a project activity.
>
> Source: Asian Development Bank.

C. The Funded Projects

IDRMF-IC-01: Greater Mekong Subregion (GMS) Flood and Drought Risk Management and Mitigation Project. This project supports strategic thrusts of the GMS Strategic Framework 2012–2022 and improving flood risk management in the GMS as part of a larger investment project undertaken by ADB in Cambodia, Lao People's Democratic Republic, and Viet Nam. In the larger investment project, ADB assists these GMS countries reduce economic losses from floods and drought by pairing upgrades in water management infrastructure with community-based DRM and enhanced regional forecasting to improve disaster preparedness. The project strengthens regional aspects of flood risk management and supports development of design criteria for flood and drought risk mitigation schemes and water control infrastructure in the Mekong Delta; assesses cross-border flood management options; and facilitates regional knowledge sharing and lessons learned from implementing project community-based DRM activities.

IDRMF-TA-02: Second Greater Mekong Subregion (GMS) Corridor Towns Development Project. This project is part of a larger ADB activity that is financing a range of infrastructure and environmental improvement investments in Cambodia, Lao People's Democratic Republic, and Viet Nam. Attention is given to corridor town development to maximize the economic benefits of increased trade and traffic flows along the major corridors in the GMS. The project supports the larger work program by establishing the basis for the proposed investments and capacity-building activities. The project is implemented in towns in Cambodia, Lao PDR, and Viet Nam.

IDRMF-TA-03, IDRMF-TA-06 / TA-8570: Support to Community-Based Disaster Risk Management (CBDRM) in Southeast Asia. These projects support innovative pilot subprojects on strengthening community disaster resilience and to facilitate peer-to-peer learning among local governments and community-based organizations on disaster resilience; and develop guidance on scaling up community

Table 1: Matrix of Integrated Disaster Risk Management Fund Activities

IDRM Fund Output → Project Title (+ Application Number) ↓	Output 1: Enhanced risk identification and analysis	Output 2: Increased investment in DRR	Output 3: Improved access to DRF solutions including for the poor and, particularly, poor women	Output 4: Scaling up of community-based and gender-focused approaches	Output 5: Increased regional cooperation of IDRM	Output 6: Enhance knowledge and tools for IDRM	Publications, Videos
IDRMF-IC-01: Greater Mekong Subregion Flood and Drought Risk Management and Mitigation Project	●			●	●		
IDRMF-TA-02: TA8425 Second Greater Mekong Subregion Corridor Towns Development Project	●	●					
IDRMF-TA-03 IDRMF-TA-06 TA8570 Support to Community-Based DRM in SEA			●	●		●	●
IDRMF-DC-02 Review of Policy and Practice Supporting Community-Based Disaster Resilience Implementation Interventions				●			●
IDRMF-TA-04 IDRMF-TA-08 TA8812 Enhanced Use of Disaster Risk Information for SEA Decision-Making	●	●	●		●	●	●
IDRMF-DC-03 TA8868 Strengthening Disaster Resilience in Selected Urban Areas	●	●			●		

continued on next page

Table 1 continued

IDRM Fund Output → Project title (+ application #) ↓	Output 1: Enhanced risk identification and analysis	Output 2: Increased investment in DRR	Output 3: Improved access to DRF solutions including for the poor and, particularly, poor women	Output 4: Scaling up of community-based and gender-approaches	Output 5: Increased regional cooperation of IDRM	Output 6: Enhance knowledge and tools for IDRM	Publications, Videos	Meetings, Forums, Workshops
IDRMF-TA-05 TA8867 Strengthening Disaster Risk of Small and Medium Enterprises in SEA	●	●				●		
IDRMF-TA-07 TA8536 Regional Knowledge Forum on Post-Disaster Recovery		●				●	●	●
IDRMF-DC-04 Strengthening City Disaster Risk Financing			●			●		●
IDRMF-DC-05 IDRMF-DC-06 Support to Implementation of ASEAN AADMER		●			●			●
IDRMF-DC-07 Dissemination of Knowledge and tools for IDRM		●	●			●	●	●
IDRMF-DC-08 Regional Workshop on Gender-Focused Investments in Climate and Disaster Resilience				●				●
IDRMF-DC-09 6th Asia-Pacific Climate Change Adaptation Forum		●				●	●	●
IDRMF-TA-09 TA9728 Scoping Community Resilience Partnership Program		●		●				●

AADMER = ASEAN Agreement on Disaster Management and Emergency Response, ASEAN = Association of Southeast Asian Nations, DC = direct charge, DRF = disaster risk finance, DRM = disaster risk management, DRR = disaster risk reduction, IDRM = integrated disaster risk management, IDRMF = Integrated Disaster Risk Management Fund, SEA = Southeast Asia, TA = technical assistance.

Source: Asian Development Bank.

resilience through government pro-poor development programs, such as social protection and community-driven development. Locations of subprograms include the Philippines, Viet Nam, and an ASEAN project (covering Indonesia, Lao People's Democratic Republic, the Philippines, Thailand, and Viet Nam); as well as assisting the Government of Myanmar develop a national framework for community disaster resilience.

IDRMF-DC-02: Review of Policy and Practice Supporting Implementation of Community-Based Interventions to Strengthen Disaster Resilience in Southeast Asia. This project covers Cambodia, Indonesia, Lao People's Democratic Republic, the Philippines, and Viet Nam; and reviews policy and practice landscapes supporting community-based disaster resilience interventions to guide governments and development partners on strengthening disaster resilience at the community level which can be scaled up through regular development interventions. The project is linked to the CBDRM project outlined in IDRMF-TA-03 and IDRMF-TA-06 by providing an overview of current community-based interventions to strengthen disaster resilience, challenges in implementation and achievements; a review of the policy landscape that supports community-based interventions; and identifying possible opportunities for scaling up implementation of small-scale interventions funded under IDRMF-TA-03 and IDRMF-TA-06.

IDRMF-TA-04 / IDRMF-TA-08: Enhanced Use of Disaster Risk Information for Decision-Making in Southeast Asia. These projects aim to strengthen the capacity of officials in Cambodia, Lao People's Democratic Republic, Myanmar, the Philippines, and Thailand to improve processes in risk-sensitive decision-making for public investments. The projects look at using disaster risk information for investment planning processes through strengthened systems for the collection and analysis of historical disaster data; improved understanding, communication, and awareness of disaster risk among sector and planning ministries; and improved understanding of tracking DRM-related investments.

IDRMF-DC-03 / TA 8868: Strengthening Disaster Resilience in Selected Urban Areas of Southeast Asia. This project is a scoping study to clarify priorities for regional and national actions that will enhance the enabling environment for strengthening urban disaster resilience. Recommendations from the scoping study will be used to guide ADB in developing a follow-up regional TA on urban disaster resilience, and to support ASEC in detailing specific aspects of the urban resilience-related priorities of the AADMER Work Programme. The regional review covers Cambodia, Indonesia, Lao People's Democratic Republic, the Philippines, and Viet Nam.

IDRMF-TA-05 / TA 8867: Strengthening Disaster Resilience of Small and Medium Enterprises in Southeast Asia. This project enhances the capacities of small and medium-sized enterprises (SMEs) in the Philippines, Thailand, and Viet Nam to strengthen disaster resilience and to develop longer-term actions for implementation. Project priorities are to support government agencies in the respective countries in identifying actions to strengthen disaster resilience of SMEs and help raise awareness of the need for strengthened resilience of SMEs; support in identifying actions to improve the enabling environment for strengthening the disaster resilience of SMEs; and to facilitate knowledge sharing among DMCs.

IDRMF-TA-07 / TA8536: Regional Knowledge Forum on Post-Disaster Recovery. This project provides a venue to exchange lessons from post-disaster recovery programs from both within and outside the region. It recognizes that post-disaster support is expected to remain an important area of operations over the medium term, reflecting the trend of rising disaster losses. In particular, the project enabled local and central government officials from the Philippines dealing with the immediate impact of Typhoon Yolanda to participate in a forum focusing on the critical issues related to managing the large-scale government-led post-disaster recovery and to be exposed to regional and international best practices and knowledge on recovery.

IDRMF-DC-04: Strengthening City Disaster Risk Financing. This project supports the organization of a workshop in Viet Nam to launch a report on *Strengthening Disaster Risk Financing in Viet Nam* and to engage relevant stakeholders on the next steps toward the implementation of pilot disaster risk financing (DRF) solutions, as well as to inform an exploration of the possible scope for further ADB engagement of DRF. Government officials from Indonesia and the Philippines, where parallel DRF projects are implemented, will also participate.

IDRMF-DC-05, IDRMF-DC-06: Support to the Implementation of the ASEAN Agreement on Disaster Management and Emergency Response (AADMER). These projects support transboundary and regional hazard management programs undertaken by ASEAN through its work program, established under AADMER. They also assist the ASEAN Secretariat (ASEC) to build its own capacity. One project funds an international consultant to support ASEC to implement its Build Safely program, designed to build resilience into essential infrastructure and services, an issue that was highlighted in an analysis undertaken in the IDRMF-DC-03 project. A second activity stream supports three ASEAN priorities to advance the implementation of AADMER and which involve decision makers and high-level technical staff from SEA government agencies: a Senior Executive Program of Disaster Management, an ASEAN Recovery Forum, and a regional workshop to disseminate ASEAN risk and vulnerability assessment guidelines.

IDRMF-DC-07: Dissemination of Knowledge and Tools for IDRM. This project provides resources to undertake national workshops in selected SEA nations and a regional workshop to share common lessons identified in the IDRM Fund projects. Apart from the direct objective of disseminating the outputs, the workshops will be used as a venue for further discussions on various IDRM priorities of the DMCs and the region.

IDRMF-DC-08: Regional Workshop on Gender-Focused Investments in Climate and Disaster Resilience. This project funds a regional workshop of high-level officials from selected SEA nations

to present the scope for investment projects in selected sectors that provide explicit opportunities for strengthening women's climate and disaster resilience, especially poor women; to identify concrete information and capacity needs for DMC governments to further develop such investment projects; and to explore potential financing sources.

IDRMF-DC-09: 6th Asia-Pacific Climate Change Adaptation Forum. This project supports the organizing of the Asia-Pacific Adaptation Network's flagship biennial event, the 6th Asia-Pacific Climate Adaptation Forum, held in Manila and cohosted by the Governments of Palau and the Philippines. Delegates represent national governments responsible for finance, planning, climate-sensitive and disaster-prone sectors, disaster risk management and CCA, community service organizations and women's groups, the private sector and business community, and bilateral and multilateral financial institutions.

IDRMF-TA-09 / TA 9822: Scoping of Community Resilience Partnership Program. This project enables a scoping exercise to be undertaken pertaining to the development of the Community Resilience Partnership Program (CRPP) initiated by ADB to support DMCs' scale-up resilience. The project will determine the need and nature of investments required to strengthen resilience of poor and marginalized people; identify types of investments appropriate for different sectors suitable for strengthening that resilience; and determine specific investment and processes that strengthen institutions and provide space to engage the poor and vulnerable in resilience policy- and program-related decision making.

D. Leveraging Integrated Disaster Risk Management Fund Investments

In keeping with ADB's IDRM approach to work in partnership with government agencies, regional and international organizations, bilateral funding agencies, the private sector, and civil society, the IDRM Fund supported specific disaster risk reduction programs pursued by development partners in the SEA region, especially on topics where value could be added to resilience-related areas requiring increased investment. In this way, projects developed by partners such as ASEAN, the Asian Disaster Preparedness Center, the United Nations Development Programme, and the United Nations Office for Disaster Reduction were supported. Some projects were cofinanced by development partners and provided inputs into further resilience interventions undertaken or planned by those agencies. Partnerships were strengthened through the regional meetings, forums, and workshops arranged as part of IDRM Fund activities to both further the aims of the respective project and to disseminate findings. The IDRM Fund also provided opportunities to partner with many implementing agencies.

It is important to note that what is highlighted in the following project reviews are aggregated outcomes that have relevance to the IDRM fund outputs as they pertain to developing nations in Southeast Asia as a whole and which can be built on in future activities. It does not discuss outcomes that are country- or project-specific.

II OUTPUT 1: ENHANCED RISK IDENTIFICATION AND ANALYSIS

Communities as actors of their own resilience. Communities, particularly women, need to be empowered to become more effective agents and leaders of their own resilience (photo by Asian Development Bank).

A. Projects Covered by Output 1

IDRMF-IC-01: Greater Mekong Subregion (GMS) Flood and Drought Risk Management and Mitigation Project.
IDRMF-TA-02: Second Greater Mekong Subregion (GMS) Corridor Towns Development Project.
IDRMF-TA-04, IDRMF-TA-08: Enhanced Use of Disaster Risk Information for Decision-Making in Southeast Asia.
IDRMF-DC-03: Strengthening Disaster Resilience in Selected Urban Areas of Southeast Asia.
IDRMF-TA-05: Strengthening Disaster Resilience of Small and Medium Enterprises in Southeast Asia.

B. Rationale for Output 1 in the Southeast Asia Context

Any decision to invest public resources in DRM involves trade-offs with other priorities in which the same resources could be invested. At present, most countries in SEA do not systematically identify what their hazardscape is, what is at risk, who is exposed to or how they are vulnerable from natural hazard impact, let alone to account for the cost of recurrent disaster losses. While some SEA nations attempt to collect, archive, analyze, and use their hazard data, efforts are generally inconsistent or insufficient. And where information is collected, it is not always shared, even though sharing information on hazards involves

relatively little expense because some government agencies already collect and analyze data on hazard and disaster risks. These, and other similar issues, mean that governments are poorly positioned to assess trade-offs implicit in their public investment decisions, and have difficulty justifying increased investment in DRM. As populations increase and rapid unrestrained development continues, especially in urban areas, vulnerability and risk will increase without greater efforts being made to frontload DRM through identification and analysis.

C. Summary of Key Outcomes

Generating Actionable Risk Information

(i)   Applying risk information to decision-making in development requires adapting both content and presentation of risk information to the needs of end users. This applies to both the type and presentation of risk information, including spatial (location, size, and resolution) and temporal (timing, duration, and time frames) characteristics.

(ii)   Establish compatibility between different relevant databases (e.g., land-use data, exposure data). Agree on a common scope and format in which data and information is captured. For instance, agree on geographic boundaries (e.g., administrative units, such as provinces and districts), the appropriate resolution which hazard data is represented and/or shared, and use of compatible tabular and mapping software.

(iii)	End users should be involved in risk assessment processes from initial design to output finalization. Specific risk communication strategies and methods need to take account of differences between end users in terms of information needs, risk perception, and educational background.

(iv)	Start with available risk information. Building up databases is important and time-consuming, but this need not delay preliminary analysis. For instance, even in the absence of vulnerability data, an analysis of hazard and exposure data can provide base layers to identify disaster risk hotspots (e.g., to appraise investment projects or preliminary land use planning). In the absence of data on exposed assets, technology such as earth-observation and tools such as Google Maps can fill gaps, which can then be addressed incrementally as better and more data is available to improve risk analysis and assessments.

(v)	Recognize uncertainties. Even if it is based on excellent data sets and methods, risk information still involves varying degrees of uncertainty associated with a lack of credible data or that our understanding of natural hazards and climate change is still evolving. The extent of uncertainty needs to be communicated clearly, so that end users can make fully informed, strategic decisions. This requires disclosure of scientific evidence and any judgments about the quality and relevance of the evidence to the risk assessment.

(vi)	Tap community knowledge. Communities have specific knowledge that needs to be tapped, not only to establish rounded and relevant risk information, but also to generate interest and support for risk reduction. Even the best scientific models are unlikely to fully grasp local conditions and specific factors influencing risk. Hence, qualitative, community-based assessment methods; and quantitative, scientific risk assessments can exist side by side, enrich, and even validate each other.

Key Lessons in Applying Risk Information to Development Planning Processes and Programs

(i)	The risk evaluation process is the basis for risk-informed development. Risk information requires evaluating and distinguishing risks that are unacceptable from acceptable risks. These risk-layering processes are the basis for risk-informed development planning, at national and subnational levels, and are sector-specific.

(ii)	Need for collaborative governance framework. Risk-informed development planning needs a collaborative governance framework in which public policy makers, technical or scientific experts, and private sector and civil society organizations work together with an informed public that demands investments in DRR and DRM. Attitudes need to change to reward resilient policy making and action, even if they do not generate clearly visible, short-term benefits. This is a long-term process and cannot be achieved through a one-off risk assessment or planning exercise.

(iii)	Incentives to encourage risk reduction. Changing incentive systems to reward forward-looking investments in risk reduction needs to be based on a solid understanding of how and when investment decisions are currently made. An essential question is how development progress is currently measured, by whom, and how associated indicators influence investment decision-making.

(iv)	Baseline for current disaster risk reduction investments. Risk-informed development requires a baseline of current DRR and DRM investments and necessary capacities and resources to address DRM and DRR gaps. This can help draw in individual sectors to better appreciate the relationship between their scope of work and risk reduction, and encourage collaborative risk-informed development planning frameworks that clarifies current and future roles and capacity in DRR and DRM. It can also help to prioritize and steer investments toward resilience strengthening.

(v)	There is no blueprint or strictly defined sequence to design and institute a risk-informed development planning system or capacity.

Depending on country contexts, it may be more practical to prioritize highly exposed and vulnerable geographic regions or sectors, develop sector-specific risk information assessment tools, and risk reduction and risk management solutions. Demonstrated evidence of the benefits of risk-informed planning and budgeting in one sector may then motivate other sectors. Similarly, such experience can provide generic development planning apex bodies, such as ministries of planning and finance, with guidance to develop risk-informed planning mechanisms and tools. Conversely, countries with centralized planning and stronger regulatory capacity may start the process at the level of national development planning apex bodies. In more decentralized contexts with strong urbanization trends, risk-informed development planning may focus initially on urban areas and spread to peri-urban and rural areas that share similar hazard exposure and vulnerabilities before defining intraterritorial and national planning arrangements and institutions.

(vi)   Communities need to drive risk-informed development. Regardless of the administrative systems of countries, communities are at the frontline of resilience and risk information, and risk-informed development planning needs to address the needs of vulnerable communities. This requires bottom-up and top-down communication and coordination mechanisms to (i) facilitate the flow of actionable risk information and resources including targeted DRM investments, and (ii) ensure that risk reduction solutions that work are identified, tracked, and replicated.

(vii)   Adopt adaptive pathways to deal with uncertainties. In the face of both uncertainty of risk scenarios and constrained resources, an incremental approach to climate and disaster risk reduction and management is more practical and easier to justify. The climate change community has termed the concept of "adaptive pathways" to address an uncertain future, meaning that they prioritize most likely scenarios (e.g., seasonal flooding or drought hazards), but identify alternative "pathways" and leave room for extra measures and investments if other scenarios transpire. Such an incremental approach that accommodates uncertainty, limited resources and learning may also work in the context of other hazards.

Basic Building Blocks to Create an Enabling Environment for Risk-Informed Development

(i)   Build up or strengthen the understanding of disaster risks. The understanding of disaster risks requires information on hazards, exposure, and vulnerability, which builds on various base layers including data on hazards; climate; hydrological, meteorological, geological or geophysical, and topographic data; population, assets, and other infrastructure, livelihoods, and other relevant socioeconomic characteristics; and historical disaster losses and damages. This material informs the identification of hazard-prone areas and scenarios and the establishment of georeferenced data sets on population, residential buildings, land and water resources, assets (e.g., industrial assets, crops, livestock, and others), and networked infrastructure (e.g., roads and transport, energy and electricity, drainage channels, and irrigation, among others), which are critical to establishing exposure patterns, including disaster hotspots. Together with an analysis of the vulnerability of these georeferenced elements and their replacement values, a fuller picture of the characteristics and distribution of disaster risks and the extent and likelihood of damages and losses can be established.

(ii)   Strengthen institutional procedures for ongoing collection, collation, analysis, and coordination of disaster risk data. Disaster risk correlates with dynamic factors such as migration, industrial development, urbanization, environmental degradation, climate change, and globalization. Hence, it is important (i) to strengthen data collection in relevant sectors (making sure there are comprehensive, systematic, and updated asset inventories and that damages and losses are continuously tracked), and (ii) regularly undertake risk analysis to monitor and reflect changes in disaster risk scenarios. Institutional arrangements include interorganizational memoranda and technical protocols about the collection, format, and transmission of data (including roles and responsibilities). It is essential to clearly allocate coordination and lead roles for risk assessments, and conventions for adopting risk assessment results. Regulations may be needed to clarify or standardize responsibilities, objectives, basic methodologies (including credible sources of base data), and intervals in which disaster risk assessments are to be conducted.

(iii) Ensure that relevant disaster risk information is effectively shared. Different users require different applications, scope, and resolution of disaster risk information. At the same time, it is important to build compatible databases and information hubs that can be easily accessed by potential end users.

(iv) Ensure disaster risk information is effectively communicated. Different communication strategies and methods are needed to reach user groups ranging from politicians, administrators, technicians, and private households. Methods need to address current risk perceptions, communication preferences, educational background, economic status, and possible social or gender barriers to accessing information. Grassroots organizations, media, educational establishments, and local governments can act as key disseminators and multipliers of disaster risk information. Partnerships with private sector agencies, such as internet providers, mobile phone companies, and insurance companies can further disseminate disaster risk information.

(v) Strengthen incentive systems for a collaborative risk governance framework. Risk-informed development requires the willingness of multiple actors (government, private, civil society) and sectors to share information and resources, adjust their own plans and programs to achieve overarching resilience objectives, and adhere to agreed-on standards and codes. Competition for limited resources or for visibility can inhibit such cooperation. Therefore, incentives that reward cooperation and participation in risk-informed development need to be designed and complemented by effective sanctions for the breach of agreed-on standards and regulations. Incentives that work are very context-specific,

but good methods for incentive-driven, cooperative risk governance now exist.

(vi) Define roles and strengthen capacities of development planning apex bodies. Development planning apex bodies (e.g., ministries of planning and finance) have key roles in facilitating the design, appraisal, and implementation of risk-informed development plans, programs, and investment projects. While the roles of these entities differ from country to country, these ministries can play crucial roles in translating resilience ambitions into longer midterm and annual development plans and budgets to coordinate risk-informed planning within and across sectors, and track and monitor the achievement of risk reduction objectives.

(vii) Communities as actors of their own resilience. Risk-informed decision-making for development ultimately needs to strengthen the resilience of vulnerable communities. Communities, particularly women, need to be empowered to become more effective agents and leaders of their own resilience. Strengthening disaster risk awareness and information helps communities to identify risk reduction priorities, act upon these priorities and ask for relevant support. Informed communities can play a pivotal role in monitoring and enforcing risk reduction norms, codes, and regulations. The integration of community DRR and DRM concerns into government policy and plans requires stronger risk governance and administrative capacity at district levels (especially in disaster risk hotspots). However, bottom-up planning processes need to ensure communities can access technical support to design, implement, and monitor risk reduction measures.

D. Areas for Further Consideration

(i) Strengthening capacity and enhancing DRM knowledge through development processes—such as land use planning—and in better financial management of the residual disaster risk through DRF. This capacity is specifically required in urban areas where rapid development is outpacing existing urban planning processes.

(ii) The need to strengthen such capacity and enhance knowledge in the context of regional cooperation is urgently required, especially recognizing the significant risks from transboundary hazards.

(iii) Development of technical tools for risk assessment and risk mapping, as line ministry and local government staff require greater understanding about how to integrate these comparatively new measures into disaster risk reduction and CCA.

Box 2: Regional Conference on Risk-Informed Development

Attended by more than 100 participants from 10 countries and development partners, the conference in Bangkok (27–29 August 2018) focused on the application of disaster risk information in national development planning, urban development, agricultural development, and disaster risk financing. The conference was organized by ADB with financial support from the Government of Canada and in partnership with the Asian Disaster Preparedness Centre (ADPC), German Corporation for International Cooperation (GIZ), Regional Integrated Multi-Hazard Early Warning System for Africa and Asia (RIMES), United Nations Development Programme (UNDP),United Nations Economic and Social Commission for Asia and the Pacific (UNESCAP), and United Nations Office for Disaster Risk Reduction (UNDRR). Key lessons in three critical areas for achieving risk-informed development were highlighted:

I. **Key Lessons in Generating Actionable Risk Information**
- (i) Adapt risk information to the needs of end users.
- (ii) End users need to be involved in risk assessment processes from their initial design to the finalization of outputs.
- (iii) Start with available risk information.
- (iv) Recognize uncertainties.
- (v) Tap community knowledge.
- (vi) Standardize risk assessment methods.

II. **Key Lessons in Applying Risk Information to Development Planning Processes**
- (i) Risk evaluation forms the basis for risk-informed development.
- (ii) A collaborative governance framework is required.
- (iii) Incentives to encourage risk reduction are important.
- (iv) Baselines on current disaster risk reduction investments are required.
- (v) No single blueprint to institute risk-informed development.
- (vi) Communities need to drive risk-informed development.
- (vii) Adopt adaptive pathways to deal with uncertainties.

III. **Building Blocks to Create an Enabling Environment for Risk-Informed Development**
- (i) Build or strengthen the understanding of disaster risks.
- (ii) Strengthen institutional arrangements for the ongoing collection, collation, analysis, and coordination of disaster risk data.
- (iii) Ensure that relevant disaster risk information is effectively shared.
- (iv) Ensure disaster risk information is effectively communicated.
- (v) Strengthen incentive systems for a collaborative risk governance framework.
- (vi) Define roles and strengthen capacities of development planning apex bodies.
- (vii) Communities should be the primary actors in securing their own resilience.

ADPC = Asian Disaster Preparedness Centre.
Source: Asian Development Bank.

III OUTPUT 2: INCREASED INVESTMENT IN DISASTER RISK REDUCTION

Women-focused investments to build climate and disaster resilience. Beneficiaries of the Conditional Cash Transfer (4Ps) program of the Philippines (photo by Asian Development Bank).

A. Projects Covered by Output 2

IDRMF-TA-02: Second Greater Mekong Subregion Corridor Towns Development Project.
IDRMF-TA-04, TA-08: Enhanced Use of Disaster Risk Information for Decision-Making in Southeast Asia.
IDRMF-DC-03: Strengthening Disaster Resilience in Selected Urban Areas in Southeast Asia.
IDRMF-TA-05: Strengthening Disaster Resilience of Small and Medium Enterprises in Southeast Asia.
IDRMF-DC-08: Regional Workshop on Gender-Focused Investments in Climate and Disaster Resilience.
IDRMF-DC-09: 6th Asia-Pacific Climate Change Adaptation Forum.
IDRMF-TA-09: Scoping of Community Resilience Partnership Program.

B. Rationale for Output 2 in the Southeast Asia Context

Sustainable action to mainstream disaster resilience into overall development frameworks are in the early stages. Overall, expenditure in support of DRM relative to gross domestic product and total budget expenditure is low in SEA nations even though disaster losses are rising with the increasing pace of development. However, many officials involved in public investment planning recognize that if efforts to achieve the Sustainable Development Goals are to have long-term sustainable impacts, increased public investments will be needed to reduce disaster risk, and improve planning and regulation to create a more favorable environment encouraging the private sector and communities to engage in risk reduction activities. With the increasing risks and frequencies of natural hazards, there is a need to better assess DRM in all major projects, investments, and budget lines. As the costs resulting from disaster impacts and recovery or reconstruction increase, there is a need to preemptively finance DRR and prepare for climate change impacts. Activities such as hazard and risk analysis, developing early warning systems, and building resilience require investments and cooperation across all sectors.

C. Summary of Key Outcomes

Recommendations from a DRM public expenditure and institutional review include:
(i) Provide capacity building on all aspects of the project cycle at ministries of finance, sector ministries, and agencies. Finance ministries should have a clear understanding of cross-sector linkages and benefits of DRM investments that build resilience and minimize post-disaster costs. Sector ministries should get capacity building to ensure DRM is mainstreamed into policies, activities, and projects.

(ii) Conduct research to determine the appropriate level of DRM expenditure in relation to national hazard risks. This includes analysis of regional and global DRM expenditure, identification of best practices from elsewhere for allocating resources to DRM, and better understanding how DRM expenditure are measured and monitored.

(iii) Revise project planning cycles and appraisal processes to include DRM. Have budget submissions or capital investment proposals include an outcome/output matrix of the contribution of the investment expenditure to cross-cutting issues such as DRM, climate change, and the environment. This can be part of a standard Environmental Impact Assessment submission. Using a matrix, ministries of finance can be supported with capacity building to devise a weighting system to for allocating budget resources.

(iv) Introduce a budget-tagging system for DRM into the annual budget process.

Strengthening Urban Disaster Resilience in Southeast Asia

(i) Strengthening urban resilience requires a balance between approaches that minimize hazard impact through better urban management and maintenance of existing disaster reduction measures, and far-sighted approaches that builds resilience for future hazards by investing in new infrastructure or altering the urban landscape. It also requires a combination of measures that embed disaster resilience in business-as-usual mode and targeted investments that explicitly manage disaster risk.

(ii) Understanding urban resilience requires looking at city-level governance in terms of mandates, resources, and capacity. However, focusing on city government alone is insufficient, given that subnational governments are almost never fully autonomous and the extent of decentralization in Southeast Asia countries varies significantly.

Technical Guideline on Typhoon-Resilient Low-Income Housing

Recognizing the limited engagement of trained building professional engineers and architects in the design and construction of low-income housing, the guideline targets three key stakeholders typically involved in housing design and construction: (i) local officials, (ii) local contractors, and (iii) homeowners. Based on globally-accepted resilience qualities, the guideline recommends practical design options to strengthen the key parts of housing—foundation, walls, and roofs. The guideline is now used by Da Nang City, Viet Nam in post-disaster reconstruction of 130 houses with funding from the Nordic Development Fund. The Da Nang City government requested relevant technical departments to apply the guideline in the government housing program for the poor.

Women-Focused Investments

Women-focused investments in climate and disaster resilience require coordination and planning among ministries and national agencies of planning and finance, women and development, sector development, DRM, and CCA. Several core principles should be kept in mind to guide investments in women's resilience to natural hazards and climate change:

(i) Investments must address structural inequalities between men and women that lead to the persistence of women's chronic vulnerabilities.

(ii) Investments should recognize and promote women's existing capacities, as well as build their resilience by strengthening their capacity to adapt to, anticipate, and absorb the impacts of natural hazards, including those influenced by climate change and variability.

(iii) Investments must bring benefits to women and not just cobenefits, or unwanted burden.

(iv) Investments should be designed and implemented by women to be the primary beneficiaries and/or users.

(v) Investments should seek to generate financial returns, where possible.

(vi) Investments should seek to create transformational change.

D. Areas for Further Consideration

Strengthening Urban Disaster Resilience in Southeast Asia

(i) To keep urban planning ahead of rapid urbanization in SEA, it is recommended to: (i) establish urban governance structures that allow forward planning for urban growth, such as redrawing city boundaries to reflect actual and projected urban expansion and allow a holistic approach to building metropolitan-wide resilience; (ii) create and strengthen planning mandates for metropolitan lead authorities in large cities covering multiple municipalities; (iii) establish mandates and resources for longer-term integrated advance planning for land zoning, roads, and other urban developments; and (iv) revise urban planning laws and policies to ensure land zoning and building and construction codes take account of climate and disaster risk, and that the location or style of new developments do not increase hazard exposure.

(ii) To build resilience in everyday urban governance, it is recommended to: (i) address gaps and overlap in urban governance structures that inhibit building resilience by clarifying legislative mandates and resource allocations for city governance as between national and subnational levels; (ii) facilitate clustering for municipalities to jointly provide services and manage hazards by reviewing financing and contractual capabilities, including creating joint venture legal entities (solid waste management, river pollution, flood mitigation); (iii) establish institutional mandates and financing mechanisms to support mainstreaming DRR and CCA into urban planning and environmental management; and (iv) go beyond allocation of budget reserves for disaster relief and response to include options for financing residual risks through insurance of government assets, parametric insurance solutions, and risk-pooling schemes for groups of national governments or subnational governments.

(iii) To share benefits from the private sector without creating new risks, it is recommended to: (i) establish mechanisms to ensure risk from large private developments is costed and reduced to ensure allowance for sharing of the benefits of private investment rather than adding net risks to the urban environment; and (ii) institutionalize guidelines and procedures to ensure infrastructure projects that use the public–private partnership modality are not only consistent with the government's public investment program, but that these projects comply with the environmental planning and assessment requirements, including project-specific environmental impact assessments.

(iv) To strengthen budget and planning linkages to support urban resilience, it is recommended: (i) that in national and local development planning integrate risk analysis in the preparation of land use plans to anchor the spatial dimension of the development plan; (ii) to identify targeted public investment projects whose primary objective is to reduce risks guided by hazard maps and risk assessments; (iii) to incorporate upgraded structural design standards to ensure public infrastructure will withstand stronger typhoons, earthquakes, or increased population pressure; (iv) to embed resilience in nontargeted public investment by locating these projects in safer zones or including design measures to strengthen resilience; (v) to incorporate disaster risk considerations in standard cost–benefit analysis of public investment projects; and (v) in the budget process, to include tracking public expenditures on risk reduction and post-disaster response.

Enabling Resilience

Instruments to unlock domestic finance need to be developed and explored, not solely from the central government, but also through the contribution of local government, communities, and local groups—including in-kind contributions—to ensure ownership and sustainability of actions.

Women-Focused Investments

Further studies are required to provide more in-depth, country- and sector-specific lists of women-focused investments to build climate and disaster resilience, which are specific to the given socioeconomic, cultural, and environmental context and the policy environment within which these investments are designed and implemented.

Box 3: Enhancing the Cambodia Disaster Loss and Damage Information System with Road Sector-Related Disaster Data

National disaster databases often do not include sector-specific damage and loss data; hence, damage and loss figures are underestimated and the case for greater investment in disaster risk reduction understated. In Cambodia, the road inventory systems of the Ministry of Public Works and Transportation (MPWT) and Ministry of Rural Development (MRD) lacked information on historical flood levels of roads. Through this project, road sector-related disaster data was integrated into the Cambodia Disaster Loss and Damage Information System (CAMDi) to support road sector planning and decision-making. The improved CAMDi contains variables that match the road inventory systems of the MPWT and MRD (road types, pavement types, culverts, and bridges) that were submerged, damaged, or destroyed in disasters. An agreement was reached on regular collection and reporting of road sector-related disaster data between the MPWT, MRD, and the National Committee for Disaster Management, which maintains and hosts CAMDi online. This systematic collection, recording, and analysis of road sector-related disaster data is useful for planning, priority setting, budgeting, and decision-making for road maintenance and rehabilitation, and upgrading, as well as monitoring and evaluation. However, capacity development of MPWT, MRD, and subnational administration officials needs to be strengthened to enhance coordination with the National Committee for Disaster Management and ensure that CAMDi becomes a principal tool in road planning and decision-making.

Source: Asian Development Bank.

IV OUTPUT 3: IMPROVED ACCESS TO DISASTER RISK FINANCE, INCLUDING THE POOR AND, PARTICULARLY, POOR WOMEN

Mangyan, indigenous minority group. Recurring disasters continue to erode development gains, preventing communities and countries from reaching development goals (photo by Asian Development Bank).

A. Projects Covered by Output 3

IDRMF-TA-03, TA-06: Support to Community-Based Disaster Risk Management in Southeast Asia.
IDRMF-TA-04, TA-08: Enhanced Use of Disaster Risk Information for Decision-Making in Southeast Asia.
IDRMF-DC-04: Strengthening City Disaster Resilience.
IDRMF-DC-08: Regional Workshop on Gender-Focused Investments in Climate and Disaster Resilience.

B. Rationale for Output 3 in the Southeast Asia Context

Often, already limited development funds are diverted to rebuilding disaster-impacted social and economic infrastructure instead of addressing the needs for which they were intended. Recurring disasters continue to erode development gains, preventing communities and countries from reaching development goals. The financial management of disaster risk is in its infancy in most SEA nations. Disaster risk financing is based on the premise that anticipating and planning for financial consequences of natural hazards will place government—both national and local—in a stronger, more resilient, and more predictable position, supporting timely post-

disaster relief, early recovery, and reconstruction efforts. Urban areas typically face particularly high disaster risk, reflecting the concentration of people, assets, infrastructure, and economic activities. City governments also face significant challenges in securing adequate resources for timely disaster recovery and reconstruction, thereby accentuating the indirect economic and social impacts of direct physical losses.

C. Summary of Key Outcomes

World's First City Disaster Insurance Pool

(i)   The IDRM Fund supported the Government of the Philippines in designing the world's first city disaster insurance pool, offering parametric insurance for earthquake and typhoon cover to 10 pilot cities. The pooled insurance arrangement will help address the significant financing gap city governments face for rapid post-disaster financing, at the same time, reducing the cost of premiums by diversifying risk and absorbing the first layer of loss from pool reserves, and, in turn, reducing the amount of reinsurance required to protect the pool.

(ii)   The city disaster insurance pool was carefully structured to ensure city governments can afford premiums, and that the pool can honor timely pay-outs and is financially sustainable. Pay-outs are funded by a combination of pool capital, initially established through seed capital, and reinsurance protection purchased from domestic and international markets.

(iii)   There is considerable potential to develop similar schemes for other countries in Southeast Asia and regional presentations have generated wide interest in the scheme, particularly in Indonesia.

Solutions to Strengthen Financial Resilience of Poor

(i)   A microfinancing scheme to support rapid recovery of clients in the aftermath of disasters proposes a combination of portfolio insurance for microfinance institutions (MFIs) against extreme weather events and an emergency liquidity facility to be made available after a climate-related disaster. Testing the feasibility of the concept was undertaken in Myanmar. Consultations with MFIs in Myanmar confirmed significant general liquidity constraints to expand microfinance lending in the country and a clear consensus among MFIs regarding the specific need to develop contingent financing arrangements to enable them to meet additional demands for post-disaster recovery lending.

(ii)   MFIs are typically able to absorb write-offs, waive interest payments, reschedule outstanding loans, and meet death payments through existing mechanisms, but limited availability of additional capital prevents them from rapidly scaling up operations to meet additional borrowing requests. Lack of affordable fresh financing can potentially lead to delayed recovery, reduced revenue-generating livelihood opportunities, and/or to an increase in borrowing from informal moneylenders and increased indebtedness.

(iii)   The project in Myanmar will help the design of a not-for-profit contingent disaster liquidity facility for MFIs in Myanmar. The facility will be designed as a revolving fund offering contingent loans to MFIs for on-lending to disaster-affected clients for recovery purposes at near-zero interest rates (covering administrative costs and risk of default only).

D.   Areas for Further Consideration

To secure the implementation of city DRF solutions, several measures need to be addressed, starting with the resolution of outstanding legal, regulatory, and financial challenges. A suitable way forward could be to work with a state government to establish a city disaster insurance pilot initiative, including some initial premium funding support.

Box 4: Philippine City Disaster Insurance Pool

The Philippine City Disaster Insurance Pool (PCDIP) was carefully structured to ensure city governments can afford premiums (via flexibility in choosing their cover), and that the pool is able to honor pay-outs in a timely manner and is financially sustainable over the long term. Pay-outs will be funded by a combination of pool capital, initially established through seed capital; and reinsurance protection purchased from local and international markets. The Government of the Philippines will provide the initial pool capital, which is expected to secure a sovereign loan from ADB for this purpose. This will be supplemented by retained profits should the PCDIP benefit from years of low disaster loss. The level of reinsurance purchased each year will be driven by the level of risk transferred to the pool by the cities, available capital in the pool, the price of reinsurance from traditional reinsurance and/or capital markets and, crucially, the level of protection PCDIP requires.

Benefits of the Philippine City Disaster Insurance Pool:
(i)   Fiscal resilience of the cities bolstered;
(ii)   Financially sound budget utilization in a risk transfer instrument with predictable pay-out expectations;
(iii)   Allows cities to become more self-sustaining in managing disaster risks and repairing critical infrastructure and assets;
(iv)   Quicker local economic recovery;
(v)   A solution to narrow the funding gap between available resources and post-disaster response costs for severe events; and
(vi)   Cities enjoy the many benefits of a pool structure, including diversification, economies of scale, and knowledge sharing.

Source: Asian Development Bank.

V OUTPUT 4: SCALING UP OF COMMUNITY-BASED AND GENDER-FOCUSED APPROACHES

Peer-to-peer learning. The consolidation and transfer of knowledge among local governments, community-based organizations, and organized groups of grassroots women is critical for strengthening community resilience and scaling up implementation (photo by Asian Development Bank).

A. Projects Covered by Output 4

IDRMF-IC-01: Greater Mekong Subregion (GMS) Flood and Drought Risk Management and Mitigation Project.

IDRMF-TA-03, TA-06: Support to Community-Based Disaster Risk Management in Southeast Asia.

IDRMF-DC-02: Review of Policy and Practice Supporting Implementation of Community-Based Interventions to Strengthen Disaster Resilience in Southeast Asia.

IDRMF-DC-08: Regional Workshop on Gender-Focused Investments in Climate and Disaster Resilience.

IDRMF-TA-09: Scoping of Community Resilience Partnership Program.

B. Rationale for Output 4 in the Southeast Asia Context

Climate change and disaster risk pose serious threats to inclusive sustainable development in SEA nations. It is at the local level that the adverse effects are most felt through loss of life, assets, livelihoods, and well-being. Risks are likely to increase in magnitude and complexity when combined with other developmental challenges, such as growing inequality, continuing environmental degradation, inadequate social services, and infrastructure deficits. If efforts to reduce poverty in SEA nations are to be sustained, strengthening disaster and climate resilience should be one of the core strategies of poverty reduction and overall development policies. Investments are needed to reduce risk by improving the design, construction, and maintenance of household and community assets and local infrastructure; and strengthening resilience of livelihoods and associated skills. Community-based development projects are investments that build resilience by targeting the most vulnerable; tapping local knowledge, capacities and resources; and focusing on a combination of structural and nonstructural measures to produce multiple benefits over different timeframes. Local communities vulnerable to climate change and disasters can be empowered to lead action on strengthening household and community resilience. Embedded within strategies to build more resilient communities must be an underlying premise of empowering marginalized populations, especially women. With disaster losses increasing in the region, and with the expected increase in intensity and frequency in some areas of climate extreme events, the need for investments aiming at strengthening disaster resilience at the community level will increase in the future, requiring a common understanding and approach among governments and their partners to ensure large-scale implementation with a sustainable impact.

While the engagement of local governments and grassroots organizations—such as women and youth groups—will be crucial in identifying the needs of vulnerable populations and addressing the root causes of vulnerability through community infrastructure, livelihoods, and social protection, there is also a need to support governments to scale up implementation of such investments.

C. Summary of Key Outcomes

Strengthening Local Resilience

(i)   There are critical needs to scale up investments that aim at strengthening resilience of the poor and vulnerable populations. These investments should include a suite of measures to help reduce risk, strengthen adaptive capacity, and manage residual risk. Social protection programs (as evident from experiences in India and the Philippines) can contribute to resilience in the household and local economy. Its contribution is dependent on types of hazards households are exposed and sensitive to; and the type and combination of instruments (social assistance, public works, social insurance) used to deliver social protection.

(ii) So too, community-driven development projects (as evident from experiences in Indonesia and the Philippines) provide opportunities for vulnerability reduction through understanding of localized risks.

(iii) Providing devolved flexible funding also allows communities to decide how resources should be spent. Experiences demonstrated the importance of subsidiarity of decisions—where local governments and communities with devolved responsibilities have the authority to allocate resources—resilience outcomes were higher.

(iv) Equally important are government reforms and accompanying investments to roll out decentralization. It advances principles of participation, inclusiveness, transparency, accountability, and flexibility, which are key for strengthening resilience. However, it is crucial to have a convergence between these investments, i.e., combining instruments with households, community, and local government focus.

(v)   Experiences show that inclusive processes between households, communities, and local governments are effective at identifying transformational resilience-building investments and generating cobenefits, including empowerment of women and vulnerable populations.

Scaling Up Grassroots Women-Led Solutions for Strengthening Resilience

Although the desired outcomes of many initiatives can only be demonstrated once local governments allocate resources for disaster risk reduction-related needs, the process of engaging community-based women organizations, building community capacity to assess disaster risk in a participatory manner, prioritizing needs, and engaging with local governments, nevertheless, has more immediate impacts in contributing to the empowerment of communities and the most vulnerable.

Scaling Up Community Resilience through Social Protection Programs

(i)   The importance of strengthening climate and disaster resilience through social protection programs lies in both how social protection programs can introduce ex ante measures to reduce risk and strengthen adaptive capacity of poor households and vulnerable populations, as well as provide ex post measures to facilitate effective post-disaster response and recovery.

(ii) The key considerations critical for social protection programs (primarily social assistance programs) to deliver on resilience outcomes include (i) improving targeting of beneficiaries by using climate and disaster risk information, (ii) adopting integrated solutions to reduce risk and strengthen adaptive capacity, (iii) introducing flexible design features to strengthen the program's shock responsiveness, and (iv) securing financial resources needed for social protection programs to deliver on resilience.

D. Areas for Further Consideration

Urgent actions are required to strengthen community resilience because large numbers of people continue to be affected by natural hazard impacts and economic losses continue to rise. Three key actions requiring attention are:

(i)   **Scaling Up**. The integration of disaster and climate risk management into wider community-driven development; involving communities in investment decision-making; and the design, implementation, and monitoring of development initiatives are urgently required to expand opportunities for strengthening community resilience and delivering solutions at a scale necessary to achieve impact.

(ii)   **Innovations**. Innovative solutions are required to strengthen community resilience—solutions that (i) reduce the underlying causes of vulnerability; (ii) build on available knowledge and practice within communities; and (iii) ensure access to services, including financial services, by the most vulnerable.

(iii) **Peer-to-peer learning**. The consolidation and transfer of knowledge through peer-to-peer learning among local governments, community-based organizations, and organized groups of grassroots women is critical for strengthening community resilience and scaling up implementation.

Box 5: Recommendations for Investing in Community-Led Strategies for Resilience

Experiences gained from the project *Closing the Gap: Empowering Women to Link Community Resilience Priorities to Decentralized Development* highlight four community-led strategies pertinent to developing economies in the Southeast Asia region and their development partners, especially international financial institutions. These strategies were applied by grassroots women's organizations to advance resilience in Indonesia, the Philippines, and Viet Nam. What is key is that communities tried and tested the strategies to advance resilient development and, in many cases, attracted resources and recognition from local, subnational, and national governments. Though led by grassroots women's organizations, these strategies are not focused exclusively on women, but also aim to improve the lives of their families and communities.

The strategies demonstrate that grassroots women's organizations are:
(i)   using community-led risk mapping as entry points for communities to identify and address climate and disaster resilience priorities;
(ii)   reducing targeting errors in government-supported social protection programs;
(iii) influencing decentralized decision-making to drive demand for community priorities for climate and disaster resilience; and
(iv)   using flexible funds to promote climate and disaster resilience practices that address underlying risks and attract government support for resilience building.

While presented as four distinct strategies, together they comprise a comprehensive approach to advancing grassroots women's priorities for inclusive, sustainable, and resilient development. Success in one strategy often builds capacities and relationships that are stepping-stones to success in the other three.

The strategies are also part of an empowerment-based approach, which seeks to reconfigure relationships of power by transforming the roles of organized women's groups engaged in shaping public decision-making. In addition to negotiating and influencing resource allocations for communities, the strategies highlight grassroots women's leadership roles in claiming resources and public recognition. This empowerment-based approach shifts women's status from passive beneficiaries to stakeholders and drivers of resilient development.

Source: Asian Development Bank.

VI OUTPUT 5: INCREASED REGIONAL COOPERATION ON INTEGRATED DISASTER RISK MANAGEMENT

Managing disaster risk is not only a national concern, but also a transboundary and regional issue. Regional organizations are increasingly active in DRM, reflecting a trend of growing regional cooperation (photo by Asian Development Bank).

A. Projects Covered by Output 5

IDRMF-DC-01: Greater Mekong Subregion (GMS) Flood and Drought Risk Management and Mitigation Project.

IDRMF-TA-04, TA-08: Enhanced Use of Disaster Risk Information for Decision-Making in Southeast Asia.

IDRMF-DC-03: Strengthening Disaster Resilience in Selected Urban Areas in Southeast Asia.

IDRMF-DC-05, DC-06: Support to the Implementation of the ASEAN Agreement on Disaster Management and Emergency Response (AADMER).

B. Rationale for Output 5 in the Southeast Asia Context

The 2015 Declaration on Institutionalising the Resilience of ASEAN and its Communities and Peoples to Disasters and Climate Change addresses risk drivers such as climate change, uncontrolled urbanization, ecosystem degradation, weak governance, limited risk management capacity, and the management of urban and rural development. It underscores the necessity to align ASEAN's pillars and relevant sectors to mainstream DRR and CCA and to develop a joint work program for resilience building, developed under AADMER. The Declaration calls for accelerated investments in these areas. However, to realize the Declaration requires going beyond ASEAN's traditional engagement through

country National Disaster Management Officers. The Declaration is an opportunity to develop new partnerships with national ministries and departments involved with urban development, planning and investment, and construction. Such linkages can extend ASEC's relationships and provide technical staff with knowledge openings from cross-pillar collaboration within sectors. The *ASEAN Vision 2025 on Disaster Management* extends this and acknowledges that mechanisms established under AADMER need to be further developed. *Vision 2025* identifies key areas to advance AADMER to a people-centered, people-oriented, financially sustainable, and networked approach by 2025. However, the key to realizing these goals is strengthening the capacity of ASEC and increasing regional cooperation in IDRM.

C. Summary of Key Outcomes

Supporting Implementation of AADMER Work Programmes

(i)   Based on requests from ASEC and endorsement from the ASEAN Committee on Disaster Management Working Groups, the IDRM Fund provided support for:

*   Rolling out the implementation of the ASEAN Risk and Vulnerability Assessment Guideline of AADMER Work Programme Priority 1: Risk Aware.

- Urban DRM priorities of AADMER Work Programme Priority 2: Build Safely.
- Provision of a technical expert position for a period of 1 year to help the ASEC implement AADMER Work Programme, especially Priority 2: Build Safely.
- Implementation of community resilience-related priorities of AADMER Work Programme Priority 3: Advance.
- Development of the ASEAN Guideline on Social Protection in Disaster Recovery under AADMER Work Programme Priority 7: Recover.
- Organizing the ASEAN Recovery Forum for AADMER Work Programme Priority 7: Recover.

(ii) The IDRM Fund underwrote two consultants to assist ASEC develop AADMER Work Programme 2021–2025: a lead consultant to support drafting AADMER Work Programme 2020–2025; and a gender consultant to ensure gender considerations are reflected in the AADMER Work Programme 2020–2025.

Formulation of ASEAN Priorities on Urban Disaster Risk Reduction

(i) The IDRM Fund urban resilience scoping study on formulating recommendations for the enabling environment required to scale up urban disaster resilience helped formulate urban resilience-related priorities for the second phase of AADMER Work Programme (2016–2020).

(ii) Subsequent support was provided to implement specific urban DRR-related priorities of AADMER Work Programme (2016–2020).

Support to DRR Programs of Development Partners

(i) Support to the United Nations Development Programme (UNDP) for institutionalizing use of disaster loss databases in key sectors (e.g., roads) at high disaster risk. These databases were developed by UNDP, but typically not integrated within wider sector management databases and, hence, lack data on sector impact of disasters. The support linked these databases with wider road sector databases in Cambodia and Lao People's Democratic Republic.

(ii) Support to the Asian Disaster Preparedness Center project on strengthening resilience to small and medium enterprises in Indonesia, the Philippines, Thailand, and Viet Nam. The project provided financing incentives from the private sector to continue the business sector's capacity building on resilience.

D. Areas for Further Consideration

Options for Strengthening Urban Governance

The study on strengthening urban disaster resilience (IDRMF-DC-03) identified options to guide ASEAN priorities on urban resilience, with recommendations directed to grants or TA projects that can be added to existing or new projects, be stand-alone, or support other projects. The options are listed under four headings:

(i) Keep Urban Planning Ahead of Rapid Urbanization

Options to support country legal or institutional frameworks for urban planning and implementing resilient urban development:

Establish urban governance structures that allow forward planning for urban growth, such as:

- Redraw city boundaries to reflect actual and projected urban expansion and allow a holistic approach to building resilience on a metropolitan-wide basis (e.g., as in Phnom Penh).
  - Create and strengthen planning mandates for greater metropolitan lead authorities in large cities covering multiple municipalities (e.g., as in Metro Manila).
  - Establish mandates and resources for longer-term integrated advance planning for land zoning, roads, and other urban development.
- Revise urban planning laws and policies to ensure that land zoning and building and construction codes take account of climate and disaster risk, and that the location or style of new developments do not increase exposure of the population to hazards.

- Reduce risk in informal settlements by: (i) formally recognizing existing informal settlements by including them in geographical maps, risk mapping, and mandates of local government; (ii) participatory resettlement of communities from high-risk areas—balancing rights and risks (e.g., as in Metro Manila's riverside settlers) and/or upgrading and regularizing established informal settlements (e.g., as in Brazil's Statute of the Cities); and (iii) contributing to prevention of high-risk informal settlements by increasing investment in social housing, including by private investors (e.g., the Philippines 20% social housing requirements as a component of private developments).

From a regional cooperation perspective, options to support legal and institutional frameworks for urban planning and implementing resilient urban development:

- Take pragmatic, but deliberate steps to integrate the ASEAN Declaration on Resilience and specifically address urban resilience through cross-sector and cross-pillar approaches by establishing a cross-sector and cross-pillar working group on urban resilience within ASEAN.
- Support the ASEAN regional Urban Resilience Forum through inputs to inform thematic discussions and direct the Forum toward priority areas on urban resilience that need cross-sector and cross-pillar cooperation. Use financial instruments to complement future investments focusing on mid- and mixed-density corridor and coastal cities in the three developing economic corridors.

(ii)   Building Resilience into Everyday Urban Governance

Options to better integrate resilient approaches to everyday urban governance:

- Address gaps and overlap in urban governance structures that may currently inhibit building resilience:

  o Clarify legislative mandates and resource allocations for city governance between national and subnational levels (e.g., Vientiane).
  o Facilitate clustering for municipalities to jointly provide services and manage hazards by reviewing financing and contractual capabilities, such as creating joint venture legal entities (e.g., Metro Manila–Marikina and neighboring municipalities, solid waste management, river pollution, flood mitigation).

- Implement DRR and CCA into urban governance by strengthening investment in DRR and CCA through new and emerging legislative and institutional structures. For example:

  o Establish or revise laws, institutions, and financial allocations for DRM to ensure they are multihazard and address DRR and CCA, plus managing residual risk through effective preparedness, response, recovery, and reconstruction.
  o Include DRR and CCA in environmental laws as part of environmental assessment tools to approve new developments, such as strategic environmental assessments as the basis for land and urban zoning, and in environmental impact assessments for projects.
  o Include DRR and CCA education in DRM system laws, public education, and training mandates, to conduct community, school, and professional education on DRR and CCA.

- Establish institutional mandates and financing mechanisms to mainstream DRR and CCA into urban planning and environmental management, including:

  o Develop and/or apply existing technical tools for risk assessment and risk mapping, as line ministry and local government staff need greater understanding how to integrate these issues of DRR and CCA.
  o Establish effective institutional mechanisms to coordinate urban master planning by cross-sector between DRM

and climate change institutions and line ministries, and with local government.

- ○ Allocate additional budget for initial integration of DRR and CCA actions and added cost of compliance with new standards, as a form of targeted investment to embed these into "business as usual."
- ○ Establish budget lines earmarked for DRR and CCA in government budgets where DRR and CCA capacity is at an early stage of development for purposes of kick-starting DRR and CCA activities, particularly those related to hazard mapping, and vulnerability and risk assessments.
- ○ Develop funding mechanisms that consider varying fiscal capacities of subnational governments and their varying exposure to risks.
- Go beyond allocation of budget reserves for disaster relief and response, options for financing residual risks through:
  - ○ Insurance of government assets.
  - ○ Parametric insurance for less frequent, but highly severe risks; preconditions for governments to access this option include: (i) reform of regulatory framework to support government's use of this solution, and (ii) government's access to specialized risk modeling capability.
  - ○ Risk-pooling schemes for groups of national governments or subnational governments.

Options for specific sector initiatives to increase urban resilience:

- Building and construction. Combine legislative sanctions for noncompliance to building and zoning regulation with campaigns to create a culture of compliance through community education and specific training for the construction sector (government and private).
- Target capacity building of local authorities to develop or modify physical planning and building codes, and to implement

rigorous building approval, inspection, and certification.

- Integrated water resources management (IWRM). Review national water laws to ensure they are based on IWRM principles to better manage flooding (human risk, benefits for fisheries and agriculture), water supply (quantity, quality, distribution, wastage), wastewater management (pollution controls, longer-term impacts of water deposits), and the broader environments from which water resources are derived (river basin management, with tributaries, and underground aquifers, catchment deforestation and/or erosion, and ecological systems). This will need budgeting for new levels of coordination or new institutions, and investment in capacity building of local staff in river basin management.
- Revise legislative, institutional, and budget frameworks for water resource management to ensure IWRM principles address water supply resilience, scarcity, quality, and demand management, and the resilience of water distribution infrastructure to all hazards (e.g., seismic risk, terrorism).
- Increased investment and policy commitment to strengthen transboundary and regional agreements for river basin management and revision of intergovernmental institutions' policies and treaty provisions to emphasize all aspects of IWRM, including long-term resilience.
- Solid waste management (SWM) systems. Improvement of legislative and regulatory framework for SWM to support an integrated SWM strategy and to ensure up-to-date regulations for specific sector-related waste streams, such as hazardous wastes and e-waste.
- Strengthening inter-local cooperation arrangements among subnational governments to enable them to take advantage of economies of scale in the SWM sector, especially in the disposal aspect.
- Some regional options to better integrate a resilient approach to everyday urban governance:

○ Develop an ASEAN urban resilience framework, based on the Arup Resilient Cities Framework modified and used globally by the Rockefeller Foundation 100 Resilient Cities program.[7]

○ Cluster activities in the post-2015 AADMER Work Programme about urban resilience, under an ASEAN urban resilience framework. Focus on commitments to city-level risk assessments and integration of DRR into land use plans and building codes, including development and compliance.

(iii) Share Benefits from Private Sector without Creating New Risks
Options for ensuring that private sector developments in urban areas do not create new risks:

- Establish mechanisms to ensure that risk from large private developments is costed and reduced, to ensure they allow sharing of the benefits of private investment, rather than adding net risks to the urban environment. This requires a consistent application of large developments to environmental planning and assessment regulation, plus land zoning based on strategic environmental assessments and risk mapping, and project-specific environmental impact assessments.
- Institutionalize guidelines and actions to ensure public infrastructure projects using the public–private partnership modality are consistent with government's Public Investment Program; and comply with environmental planning and assessment requirements, and project-specific environmental impact assessments.

Regional options to ensure private sector developments in urban areas do not create new risks:

- Address risk and strengthen existing partnerships with the nongovernment and civil society sector, specifically with the AADMER Partnership Group, to capitalize on their private sector engagement.

(iv) Strengthen Planning and Budgeting Linkages
Options to stimulate investments in urban resilience and secure funds for resilience from government:

- In national and local development planning:
  ○ Incorporate the results of an analysis of the multisector impact of past disasters and ensure alternative development paths yield risk-sensitive articulation of sector goals, strategies, and projects.
  ○ Integrate risk analysis in the preparation of the land use plan which serves to anchor the spatial dimension of the development plan.
- In identification and design of public investment projects:
  ○ Identify targeted public investment projects whose primary objective is to reduce or mitigate risks guided by hazard maps and risk assessments.
  ○ Incorporate upgraded structural design standards to ensure that public infrastructure will withstand stronger typhoons, higher intensity earthquakes, or increased population pressure.
  ○ Embed resilience in nontargeted public investment by locating projects in safer zones or include measures to mitigate risks resulting from the project itself in the design of the said projects.
  ○ Include disaster risk considerations in standard cost–benefit analysis of public investment projects.

In the budget process:

- Strengthen planning–budget linkage by ensuring (i) public investment planning is used for allocating the government budget, (ii) all public investment projects included in the project implementation plan are ranked

---

[7]   Rockefeller Foundation. 2014. *City Resilience Framework*. London: Arup International Development.

in accordance with clear and transparent criteria, and (iii) the aggregate spending level authorized by the government budget is consistent with the government's medium-term fiscal framework.

- Track public expenditures on building resilience and responding to risk. If done with line agency staff, it will give them hands-on experience in working out which of their programs, activities, and projects are resilience-related, and contribute to their knowledge in embedding resilience in their future activities. The tracking exercise is also a useful tool to inform government decision-making on the appropriate balance and composition of risk reduction and post-disaster expenditure.

VII OUTPUT 6: ENHANCED KNOWLEDGE AND TOOLS FOR INTEGRATED DISASTER RISK MANAGEMENT

IDRM Fund activities to disseminate findings. A seminar explored community-led solutions for strengthening resilience and good practices on how such solutions can be scaled up through large-scale government investments (photo by Asian Development Bank).

A. Projects Covered by Output 6

IDRMF-TA-03, TA-06: Support to Community-Based Disaster Risk Management in Southeast Asia.
IDRMF-TA-04, TA-08: Enhanced Use of Disaster Risk Information for Decision-Making in Southeast Asia.
IDRMF-TA-05: Strengthening Disaster Resilience of Small and Medium Enterprises in Southeast Asia.
IDRMF-TA-07: Regional Knowledge Forum on Post-Disaster Recovery.
IDRMF-DC-04: Strengthening City Disaster Risk Financing.
IDRMF-DC-07: Dissemination of Knowledge and Tools for Integrated Disaster Risk Management.
IDRMF-DC-09: 6th Asia-Pacific Climate Change Adaptation Forum.

B. Rationale for Output 6 in the Southeast Asia Context

In addressing natural hazards, many SEA nations already raised the profile of DRR in their national development plans and strategies. The next step—the systematic integration of disaster risk (current and future) information into development programming and design, implementation, and maintenance of individual projects across all relevant sectors—has presented challenges. The reasons are complex and often rooted in difficulties to formulate and coordinate risk-informed policies, set well-defined and measurable sector-specific DRR targets, and nurture a supportive risk governance environment to implement these targets. These institutional and managerial challenges often coincide with a lack of overall knowledge of the direct and indirect socioeconomic impact of disasters and a limited understanding of contextual factors that feed into the exposure and vulnerability to natural hazards. Similarly, limited capacity in assessing DRR, identifying risk reduction opportunities and solutions, and estimating costs and benefits to integrate risk reduction measures into development fall behind overall policy intentions.

C. Summary of Key Outcomes

Enabling Conditions to Support Resilience

(i)   Uncertainty is inherent in adaptation planning and decision-making. The intrinsic variability in climate and in human, social, economic, and environmental systems impose uncertainty about what to adapt to. Similarly, the available information and knowledge is often incomplete, but this is not an excuse for inaction. It is vital to make the best use of all research and information—traditional, science-based, and risk-informed—so actions are coordinated and transformative. Information as an evidence base is crucial, but there is a need to balance action and the need for detailed scientific evidence.

(ii) Policy and governance structures must be inclusive, gender-responsive, and support communities, as well as natural and physical systems, to deliver best resilience outcomes. Only people-centered, integrated policies supported by coordinated governance systems mindful of local realities can do this.

(iii) Planning and designing actions to adapt to climate change impacts require science-based planning and the use of both traditional and modern knowledge. There is a need for better integration of CCA and DRR and an urgent imperative to improve information flow for effective planning and management. Coordination and collaboration must be improved in dealing with divergent interests and agenda among various stakeholders during both planning and implementation.

(iv) Technologies and practices must be used to support job creation, food security, life and property, and sustainable livelihoods. They should enhance resilience of both the natural and built environments.

Gender-Focused Investments in Climate and Disaster Resilience

Women-focused investments in climate and disaster resilience should possess:

(i) Investments having women as the starting point. Investments that (i) address structural inequalities between men and women that lead to the persistence of women's chronic vulnerabilities; (ii) are designed and implemented by women as the primary beneficiaries and/or users; and (iii) do not contribute to women's time, poverty, and burden of care.

(ii) Investments that generate financial returns. Women-focused investments are still investments that need to generate financial returns, besides fostering resilience, increasing gender equality, and promoting economic development. This is especially so if investments seek private sector involvement.

(iii) Investments that are transformational. Women-focused investments in climate and disaster

resilience should plan for transformational change by adopting design features that make it more likely. The literature on transformative climate investments consistently identifies four dimensions that increase the chances of interventions to activate transformational processes and achieve transformational outcomes: (i) relevance – referring to the strategic focus of interventions, improving women's resilience to the impacts of climate change and natural hazards; (ii) systemic change – referring to fundamental shifts in structures and functions of the system affecting the resilience of women; (iii) scale – referring to contextually large-scale transformation processes and impacts in relation to women's resilience; and (iv) sustainability – referring to the robustness and resilience of changes in relation to women's resilience.

Lessons on Post-Disaster Recovery

(i) Commence recovery while relief is ongoing. The overlap between the humanitarian response and early recovery and reconstruction may need to be increased to fast-track the initiation of economic recovery and reduce the overall fiscal burden of disaster. The development of ex ante financing instruments for post-disaster responses will be critical to ensure the availability of resources for timely recovery and reconstruction efforts.

(ii) Develop a strategic framework to guide recovery. A strategic framework is needed in the aftermath of a disaster. The framework should outline strategies aligned with long-term development strategies of the affected area, articulate the short- and medium-term needs across sectors and the budgetary requirements, describe regulatory and institutional reforms needed to fast-track recovery execution, and detail the role of government and nongovernment stakeholders and the coordination mechanisms.

(iii) Establish government-led institutional setup and coordination mechanisms. The choice of institutional setup to lead and coordinate recovery will differ among countries. However, events show that success rests on the political importance attached, including the selection of a credible leader, clearly defined mandates, and adequate power and authority to command actions across agencies.

(iv) Coordination is a crucial function of such setups and should strengthen—not weaken—existing government-led systems and ensure horizontal coordination across sectors and vertical coordination from local to national and international levels.

(v) Build on programs with a proven track record. Recovery requires immediate restoration of services and facilities on the ground. Using programs with a proven track record—with an established implementation structure and rules for implementation—can significantly hasten recovery. Program designs that are simple move faster compared to large and complex ones.

(vi) Build back better and strengthen resilience. Disasters offer a unique window to address root causes of vulnerability—such as improper land use zoning, poor enforcement of building codes, and gender inequality—and strengthen resilience. The "building back better" process should adopt a multihazard, systems-based, and integrated approach, factoring in current and future risks; apply engineering standards for strengthening resilience of physical assets; employ strategies and tools for pre-disaster financial planning; and strengthen capacities to manage residual disaster risk through local preparedness and business continuity management.

(vii) Involve local communities in the recovery effort. Communities want to be informed of government's plans for recovery. Since the purpose of recovery is to support affected communities and strengthen their resilience, the recovery process should give ample time and space for the voice and aspirations of the communities to be heard. Engaging local communities from day one will promote ownership of the recovery process and contribute to its success.

(viii) Strengthen local capacity, even though large-scale disasters can easily overwhelm local capacities. From assessment and planning to implementation and monitoring, local government may not possess adequate technical and financial capacity to carry out basic recovery functions and mandates. This requires abundant technical assistance to support local governments and help build a cadre of local experts.

(ix) Establish monitoring systems to improve transparency and accountability. Having a unified, web-based, and geographically referenced monitoring system accessible to all implementing agencies, local governments, and development partners is critical for successful recovery. Such a mechanism provides up-to-date information on the recovery process, pinpoints overlaps and gaps, and enables partners to strengthen synergies among their interventions.

(x) Manage expectations by making critical use of communication. As recovery is everyone's responsibility, communicating roles, goals, and progress is crucial to recovery. It is imperative that communication be consistent and comprehensive to help coordinate efforts. A robust monitoring system is needed to enable the effective communication of the process and progress toward recovery.

(xi) Adopt a phased and flexible approach. Full recovery takes time, during which different priorities may be addressed at varying times. Implementation of the recovery program requires a phased and flexible approach that allows for the program focus to be adjusted over time to meet evolving needs.

(xii) Revisit the recovery plan as information becomes available. Assess the damage and loss as quickly and efficiently as possible to inform investment decisions. Existing assessment methodologies and technical knowledge from international experience can inform initial estimates of impact. Later assessments can be started as further information, sector evaluations, and local information become available.

(xiii) Maintain a culture of urgency. Normal implementation and coordination arrangements among government agencies and their partners may not be suitable to meet the urgent and critical tasks entailed in recovery. The first 2 years of implementation in a recovery process are characterized by slow delivery amid high expectations from affected communities, especially after intensive relief efforts. Approaches beyond business-as-usual that achieve results for the most vulnerable are necessary to achieve rapid reconstruction.

(xiv) Consolidate experience into policy, planning, and financing. Recovery reveals policy issues, institutional bottlenecks, and operational hurdles that impede recovery efforts. Certain national laws, regulations, and policies can delay project implementation, such as policies on procurement, land acquisition, and the many required permits and clearances needed to start projects. Through monitoring, evaluation, and knowledge sharing, these policies can be reviewed and revisited as necessary.

Post-Disaster Recovery Risk-Informed Land Use Planning

(i)   Use probabilistic risk assessments for planning. The past or present is not a clear sign of the future, especially with hazard shifts due to climate change. It is vital to conduct probabilistic disaster risk assessments, assessing the probability of disaster impacts in each location based on multihazard scenarios of thousands of years. While technology to undertake such assessments has improved, the capacity to use results for decision-making is limited, especially in a post-disaster context.

(ii)   Strengthen synergy between micro- and macro-level planning. Micro-level planning incorporating participatory approaches is critical to gaining ownership of disaster-affected populations in recovery. Macro-level planning is crucial for infrastructure reconstruction, protecting natural resources, identifying large-scale investments to strengthen resilience, and ensuring the recovery process is aligned with long-term development objectives of the affected area. The micro- and macro-level plans should be aligned with each other to ensure there are no contradictions in measures being proposed at different levels and that the needs of the communities are reflected in the social, economic, and infrastructure plans and programs of higher levels of government.

(iii)   Be guided by the geographical characteristics of the area and natural ecosystems to establish a planning unit. Watersheds can be a critical planning unit as they view an area as a whole and recognize interconnectedness.

(iv)   Propose a package of land-use related policy measures. Different measures may be needed to tackle existing and new disaster risks. Measures such as no-build zones around environmentally sensitive areas of relocation sites are suitable for limiting the formation of new risks; and new regulations and incentives to restrict the type, density, and design of housing as part of in situ reconstruction are critical for reducing existing risk. Implementation can begin with measures that bring quick wins and move on over time, with increased availability of disaster risk information and engagement of local stakeholders, to the more difficult ones.

(v)   Gain political support, participation of disaster-affected communities and collaboration across administrative units. Implementing risk-informed land use policy measures may have economic implications. It is important to work closely with decision makers to ensure proposed policy measures have political acceptability and buy-in from major interest groups. It is critical to involve disaster-affected communities as it helps to increase ownership of plans, resolve conflicts, and, in the long run, strengthen social capital.

(vi)   Recognize linkages with the larger suite of DRM solutions. While risk-informed land use planning is critical for strengthening resilience, it is only one piece in the larger suite of DRM solutions, which includes improved hazard forecast and risk modeling, strengthened building resilience, improved preparedness planning, and strengthened financing arrangements.

(vii)   Promote a culture of pre-disaster recovery planning. Pre-disaster recovery planning is critical for speedy and effective implementation of risk-informed land use planning in a post-disaster context. This requires changing existing land use-related legislation, undertaking probabilistic disaster risk assessments at a scale that can be used for planning purposes, improving understanding of disaster risk, making disaster risk information easily available, and strengthening capacity across different administrative levels to use such information for land use planning purposes.

D. Areas for Further Consideration

Enabling Conditions to Support Resilience

(i)   There is a call for new forms of partnerships to scale up the application of existing technologies and generate new climate-smart technologies.

(ii)   Innovations, such as big data and cutting-edge information systems, should be employed to enhance resilience, as well as new media for awareness and outreach. There is scope for effective cross-learning and knowledge-sharing opportunities in using new technologies and practices for climate adaptation.

(iii) There is a need to shift from project-based approaches and embed sustainability in proposed initiatives. At the outset of the project design and implementation agreement, efforts to institutionalize the initiative will help to ensure sustainability beyond the project's lifetime.

(iv)   For seamless implementation of policies and strategies, an approach involving and consulting with all state and nonstate actors (government agencies, civil society organizations, community leaders, youth, vulnerable groups and communities, nongovernment organizations, and the private sector), should be adopted. Roles and responsibilities to undertake actions must be clearly defined and translated from broader national-level policy perspectives. A bottom-up approach in formulating policies—which recognizes the role of local institutions

and community-led initiatives and considers vulnerable communities and groups not only as beneficiaries, but as agents and drivers of change—will assist the vertical connections of actors and highlight their roles in implementing policies. This will ensure the voices of the poor and marginalized are truly integrated into policy development and involved in an inclusive governance system. There is a need for policy and governance structures to incentivize participation from the private sector, ensure supply chain readiness, and allow for direct action on the ground.

(v)   Gender equality aspects should be integrated into climate adaptation plans, strategies, and actions. This supports and strengthens existing capacities, and facilitates women's economic empowerment, and builds women's leadership and skills, particularly in plans relating to migration, resettlement, relocation, and disaster preparedness and response.

(vi)   It is important to empower migrant communities, as well as host communities and countries with policies to facilitate integration and social cohesion. It is vital to strengthen channels for these diaspora communities to contribute to sustainable development in their home countries.

(vii) There is a need to establish a knowledge management platform on gender mainstreaming in CCA. This would allow for upscaling efforts, including attracting investments in technology and data, which would assist in equipping women to build resilience in their communities, in the face of projected disasters.

Box 6: Recommendations of Policy Dialogue on Gender Issues in Disaster Risk Reduction and Climate Change Adaptation for Association of Southeast Asian Nations Countries

The policy debate on gender issues in disaster risk reduction (DRR) and climate change adaptation (CCA) for Association of Southeast Asian Nations (ASEAN) countries produced these general recommendations:

1. **Gender-responsive DRR and CCA policies**
   (i) Review and work on the adoption and/or enhanced implementation of gender-responsive national policy, legislation, action plans, programs, and monitoring and evaluation mechanisms on DRR and CCA.
   (ii) Strengthen institutional coordination across relevant ministries and/or agencies in charge of women and children, disaster management, and environment at national and subnational levels.
   (iii) Enhance policy coordination mechanisms at the national level to ensure inclusion of gender perspectives in the national agenda for DRR and CCA. Promote an enabling policy environment to facilitate the meaningful participation of women in decision and policy making at all levels on DRR and CCA issues.

2. **Resource mobilization and increased collaboration**
   (i) Urge national governments to allocate resources for gender-sensitive DRR and CCA capabilities.
   (ii) Encourage development partners, United Nations (UN) agencies, multilateral and intergovernmental organizations, civil service organizations (CSOs), the private sector, and other stakeholders to develop tools, knowledge, research, and strategies linking DRR and CCA for implementing a country-driven approach at the national level.
   (iii) Strengthen collaboration with government agencies, women's organizations, DRR and CCA authorities, CSOs working for the empowerment of women and children, the private sector, and other stakeholders in the development and implementation of gender-responsive programs and trainings on DRR and CCA that focus on vulnerable communities.
   (iv) Strengthen collaboration among ASEAN sectoral bodies to support gender DRR and CCA mainstreaming.

3. **Gender-sensitive data collection and information**
   (i) Develop gender-responsive indicators for DRR to monitor progress in mainstreaming gender perspectives in DRR and CCA. Set up gender-sensitive monitoring and evaluation database or system for sex-disaggregated data.
   (ii) Encourage sex-disaggregated data collection across relevant ministries and agencies in charge of women and children, disaster management, and environment at national and subnational levels.
   (iii) Undertake vulnerability risk assessments that apply a gender perspective to surface the different impacts of disasters and climate change on women and girls.
   (iv) Adopt an evidence-based approach to develop, implement, monitor, and evaluate gender-responsive DRR and CCA in the region, that shall include the
      • undertaking of rights-based and gender-responsive vulnerability risk assessments;
      • identification of gender-responsive indicators and setting-up a corresponding database system;
      • collection of sex-disaggregated data across ministries and agencies in charge of women and children, disaster management, and environment at the national and subnational levels.

continued on next page

Box 6 continued

4.   **Capacity development for gender mainstreaming in DRR and CCA**
    (i)   Build capacities on gender mainstreaming in DRR and CCA that is science-based, yet cognizant of
           applicable local knowledge and practices.
    (ii)   Encourage increased investment in building the capabilities and capacities of women of DRR and CCA.
    (iii) Strengthen ASEAN support on DRR and CCA gender mainstreaming specially to exchange
           best practices.

5.   **Awareness and knowledge improvements**
    (i)   Launch regional, national, and local gender-responsive campaigns to increase citizen
           DRR understanding.
    (ii)   Promote a gender-sensitive DRR and CCA training program for media organizations and partners.

Source: Asian Development Bank.

Advancing gender equity in DRM. IDRM Fund has built a case for recognizing women as agents of change in resilient development as opposed to being vulnerable. Women can lead resilience-building initiatives that aim at promoting gender equality (photo by Asian Development Bank).

A. The Integrated Disaster Risk Management Fund Outcomes

The Design and Monitoring Framework of the IDRM Fund signaled two indicators to measure achievement of the Fund's outcome of *increased access to and use of IDRM tools in Southeast Asia by key stakeholders including vulnerable groups, particularly women*. These indicators are:

(i) Increased number of IDRM projects undertaken in participating DMCs, and

(ii) Increased percentage of tools developed that are relevant and inclusive of the needs and perspectives faced by vulnerable groups, particularly women.

B. Results

Increased Number of IDRM Projects Undertaken in Participating DMCs

Contributions to this target include:

(i) Financing the project design of future ADB investments in IDRM. For example, the city disaster insurance pool will directly support the project design of a pipeline ADB investment.

(ii) Financing discrete IDRM components of larger investment grants or loans of ADB. For example, by providing grant financing to the Government

of Viet Nam to implement specific disaster risk reduction–related outputs of the regional investment project for the Greater Mekong Subregion Flood and Drought Risk Management and Mitigation Project.

(iii) Financing disaster risk assessment and capacity building in parallel to ADB's project preparatory technical assistance to influence the design of larger investment projects and make them disaster-resilient. For example, the technical assistance provided to Cambodia, Lao People's Democratic Republic, and Viet Nam as part of the project preparation for the Second Greater Mekong Subregion Corridor Towns Development Project helped institutionalize IDRM in the investment planning processes of six towns, thereby influencing the design of the larger investment project focusing on urban infrastructure. The IDRM Fund provided technical assistance to the Government of Myanmar under the Third Greater Mekong Subregion Corridor Towns Development Project helped ensure investments are disaster-resilient.

(iv) Financing ongoing regional IDRM projects of development partners and establishing their synergy with ADB's ongoing investments or priority sector, which increases the potential for future IDRM-related investments by government and ADB. For example, the technical assistance for Enhanced Use of Disaster Risk Information for decision-making in Southeast Asia, provided to the UNDP, to institutionalize the use of disaster loss databases in key sectors (e.g., roads) at high disaster risk and to have investments from ADB. Such synergy allowed the concerned road ministry and ADB to use data from the disaster loss database to inform the design of pipeline road investments and make them disaster-resilient.

(v) Financing ongoing regional IDRM programs and projects of development partners and establishing linkages with potential future investments of ADB and other development partners. For example, the outputs of the Philippine components for Strengthening Disaster Resilience of Small and Medium Enterprises in Southeast Asia fed into the design and implementation of the Government of Canada's potential bilateral support to the Government of the Philippines on strengthening resilience of small and medium enterprises. The results of the project will feed into the design of an ADB investment for rural SMEs in the Philippines.

(vi) Financing capacity building where communities, especially women, can assess and prioritize their IDRM-related needs and influence local government in the allocation of budget to related investments. For example, the pilot subproject on Closing the Gap: Empowering Women to Link Community Resilience Priorities to Decentralized Development in Indonesia and the Philippines built the capacity of community-based women organizations to work with 20 poor rural and urban communities engage with local authorities to access resources from the local development funds to implement IDRM-related needs. Although the outcome of the pilot subproject can only be demonstrated once the local government has allocated its own resources to address IDRM-related needs, the process of engaging community-based women organizations, building community capacity to assess disaster risk in a participatory manner, prioritizing needs, and engaging with

the local governments, contribute, nevertheless, to empowering the communities and the most vulnerable.

Increased Percentage of Tools Developed that are Relevant and Inclusive of the Needs and Perspectives Faced by Vulnerable Groups, Particularly Women

The IDRM Fund supported the development of various IDRM-related tools: frameworks, methodology, guidelines, and databases. The tools were selected based on (i) direct demand from stakeholders, especially vulnerable groups and particularly women (through their representatives in community-based organizations), (ii) their potential to influence increased investments in IDRM, (iii) regional commitments of governments (e.g., tools supporting the implementation of the ASEAN AADMER Work Programme), and (iv) their likely sustainability beyond the project period (e.g., linking to existing national databases).

(i) **Frameworks.** Examples include support to the Government of Myanmar to develop a National Framework for Community Disaster Resilience. The framework argues for the need for community-level investments to strengthen disaster resilience and to achieve inclusive and sustainable socioeconomic development. Based on the request from the Government of Myanmar to support implementation of the framework, ADB is now (i) in advanced stages of discussions with the Government of Canada to develop a technical assistance project to support implementation of specific components of the framework; and (ii) in discussion with the Government of Myanmar to develop a project (loan and grant) focusing on disaster-resilient rural development, including with financing from ADB's Disaster Risk Reduction Financing Mechanism under Asian Development Fund 12.

(ii) **Methodology.** Examples include support to the governments of Lao People's Democratic Republic and Thailand to develop a methodology for tracking DRM-related public expenditure. The methodology supports government agencies to better recognize tracking DRM-related expenditure, including post-disaster expenditure. Such understanding can ensure (i) that individual line agencies have sufficient resources to meet their DRM-related responsibilities, (ii) that the balance of expenditure between DRR and post-disaster response is cost-effective, and (iii) that the extent and nature of public spending on DRM is rational relative to the scale and nature of disaster risk and other demands on public resources.

(iii)   **Products.** Examples include (i) the design of a financial scheme by Vision Fund International for its microfinance institutions to support rapid recovery of their clients following disasters. The scheme has a combination of portfolio insurance for microfinance institutions against extreme weather events and an emergency liquidity facility made available in following a climate-related disaster. Based on the success of the pilot, ADB expressed interest to provide further support to develop the proposed scheme into a regional mechanism, with possible ADB investment in the scheme in due course. And (ii) the Asian Region Disaster Insurance Scheme: Philippines Post-Haiyan assisted microfinance institutions develop financial tools to support rapid recovery of their clients affected by disasters.

(iv)   **Guidelines.** Examples include (i) guidelines developed by the Huairou Commission for grassroots women's organizations to engage with local government in resilience-building measures; (ii) guidelines on scaling up community resilience measures through investments in community-driven development; (iii) guidelines on strengthening community resilience through social protection; (iv) guidelines developed by Da Nang City, Viet Nam on typhoon-resilient housing construction, to be used in a project between Da Nang City and the Nordic Development Fund to construct 180 typhoon-resistant houses in 30 communities or wards; and (v) guidelines for community-based organizations and Viet Nam women's union to integrate IDRM-related needs in local development planning and budgeting processes.

(v)   **Database.** Examples include support to UNDP to improve the national disaster loss databases in Cambodia, Lao People's Democratic Republic, and Myanmar by strengthening its linkages with sector agencies (ministries of public works in the cases of Cambodia and Lao People's Democratic Republic) and local governments (five cities in Myanmar). The sector and cities were selected keeping in mind ADB's future investments in the area.

(vi)   **Approaches.** Examples include the peer-to-peer learning initiative among community-based organizations implemented by Oxfam under IDRM Fund support to ASEAN. This initiative explored the role of social learning in strengthening climate and disaster resilience in addressing uncertainties related to the potential impacts of climate change.

Thus, the outcome indicators of the IDRM Fund were achieved, including an increased number of IDRM projects in participating countries and the growing availability of various IDRM-related tools to meet demand from various stakeholders, especially vulnerable groups and, particularly, women.

Advancing gender equity in DRM has been a priority of the IDRM Fund, with support to implement gender-focused pilots on strengthening community resilience, setting targets to ensure the participation of women in project activities, organizing policy dialogue to raise awareness and gain high-level commitment for advancing the role of women in resilience building, and developing a knowledge product on women-focused investments in climate and disaster resilience. Approximately 25% of the total fund has supported activities with gender equality as its key focus. Based on the lessons, the IDRM Fund has built a case for recognizing women as agents of change in resilient development as opposed to being vulnerable. Such a shift in focus facilitates the identification of opportunities in different sectors where women can lead resilience-building initiatives. Initiatives such as these aim at promoting gender equality while bringing transformational changes.

Table 2: Participation of Women in Key Events Organized by the Integrated Disaster Risk Management Fund

Project	Event
TA 8570: Support to Community-Based Disaster Risk Management in Southeast Asia	Policy Debate on Gender Issues in Disaster Risk Reduction and Climate Change Adaptation for ASEAN Countries
	Lessons Learned from Implementing Community-Level Interventions for Strengthening Community Disaster Resilience
	Consultation Workshop to Develop Guidance on Strengthening Community Resilience
	Regional Workshop on Strengthening Local Resilience: Investing in Communities
	Regional workshop on peer-to-peer learning
TA 8812: Enhanced Use of Disaster Risk Information for Decision-Making in Southeast Asia	National Workshop: Design of a Philippines' City Disaster Insurance Pool
	Regional workshop to develop ASEAN training course for urban planners
	Regional workshop on risk-informed public investment planning
	Regional workshop on public expenditure tracking for DRM
ASEAN-Related Events	Senior Executive Programme in Disaster Management 2017
	ASEAN Recovery Forum
	ASEAN Regional Consultation Workshop on Social Protection
	ASEAN Workshop on Resilient Recovery

ASEAN = Association of Southeast Asian Nations, TA = technical assistance.

Source: Asian Development Bank.

Supporting the DRM-related priorities of ASEAN has also been a priority of the IDRM Fund. The total direct support provided by the IDRM Fund toward the implementation of the ASEAN Agreement on Disaster Management and Emergency Response (AADMER) Work Programme amounts to approximately 11% of the total amount of allocation approved. It has supported five of the eight priority areas of AADMER. It included the provision of technical expertise as well as organization of conference, training, and workshops. The table below, which shows all eight of the AADMER Work Programme areas, demonstrates this support.

The specific format of the IDRM Fund did raise some early issues, in particular, (i) the regional (three countries) characteristic of the Fund which, at times, limited its usage within ADB, especially since most of ADB's operations focus on single countries; (ii) the approach adopted by ADB to allow civil society organizations and community-based organizations, which typically do not function at a regional level, to apply for the Fund through an umbrella regional technical assistance; (iii) the significant demand from partners to collaborate with ADB under the Fund and the need to manage expectations in view of the limited availability of resources under the Fund; (iv) the need

Table 3: Integrated Disaster Risk Management Fund Support to the ASEAN Agreement on Disaster Management and Emergency Response Work Programme Priorities

	AADMER Work Programme Priorities	Direct Support from IDRM to implement AADMER Work Programme
1	Risk Aware (Risk Assessment)	1st ASEAN Workshop to Disseminate Risk and Vulnerability Assessment Guideline
		2nd ASEAN Workshop to Disseminate Risk and Vulnerability Assessment Guideline
		Translation of ASEAN Risk and Vulnerability Assessment Guidelines
2	Build Safely (Infrastructure, Safe Schools, Urban)	Scoping of urban resilience priorities of AADMER Work Programme 2
		Development of training course on risk-sensitive urban land use planning
		Disaster risk management specialist
		Organizing workshop on infrastructure resilience
3	Advance (Communities)	Peer-to-peer learning on community resilience
4	Protect (Risk Financing, SME, Safety Nets)	No support is provided on this topic
5	Respond	Not applicable (does not match the priorities of the IDRM Fund)
6	Equip	Not applicable (does not match the priorities of the IDRM Fund)
7	Recover (Recovery, Social Protection)	Support the development of outline for ASEAN Guideline on Disaster Responsive Social Protection
		Organizing 1st ASEAN Recovery Forum
		ASEAN Workshop on Resilient Recovery
8	Lead	Organizing the third senior executive program on disaster management

AADMER = ASEAN Agreement on Disaster Management and Emergency Response, ASEAN = Association of Southeast Asian Nations, SMEs = small and medium-sized enterprises.

Source: Asian Development Bank.

for flexibility to seize time-bound opportunities and meet new demands to strengthen resilience, such as after large-scale disasters; and (v) ADB's efforts to foster partnerships by proactively encouraging joint proposals from regional partners that address critical gaps in ongoing regional programs. However, these matters were overcome with minor modifications to the Design and Monitoring Framework (such as focusing on specific outputs and ensuring that tangible results are achieved in these areas, and recognizing the regional nature of the Fund may not be the best approach for implementing certain outputs that require country-specific actions to achieve effective results), and did not detract from the very positive contribution the IDRM Fund made, not least of which was that all approved projects were demand-driven.

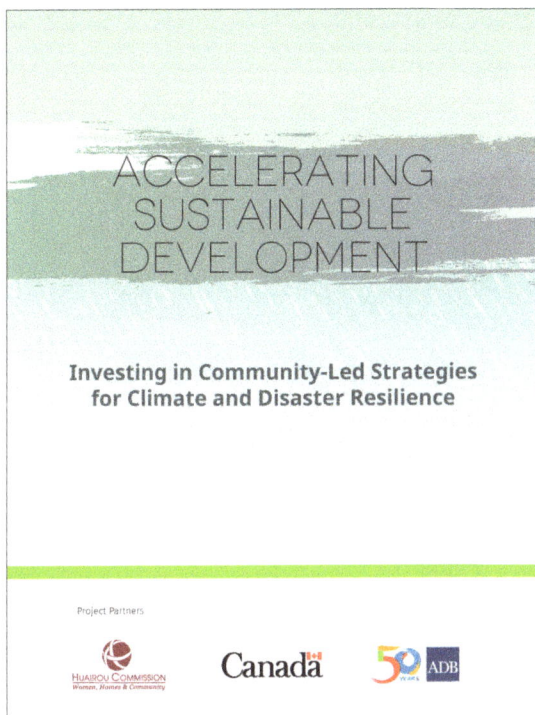

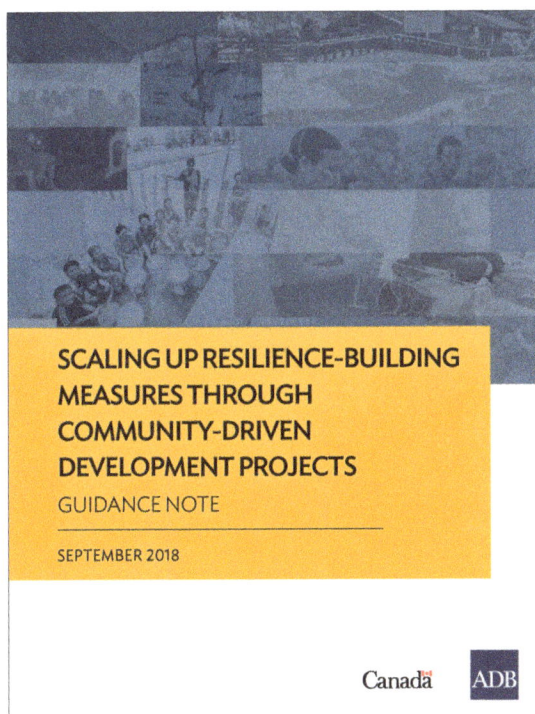

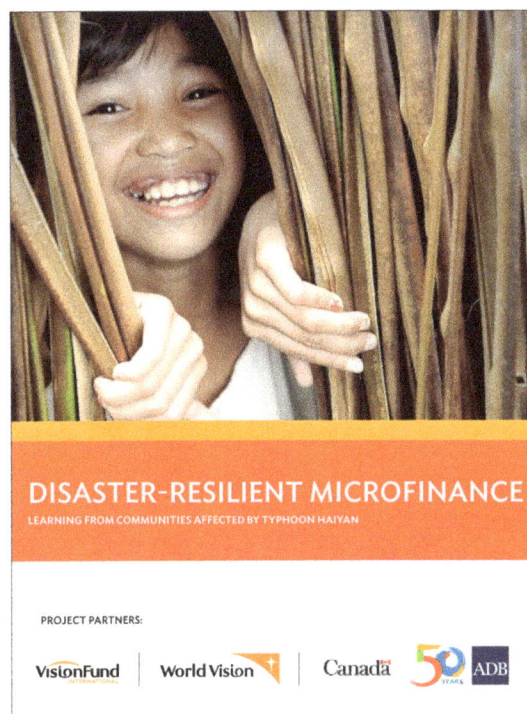

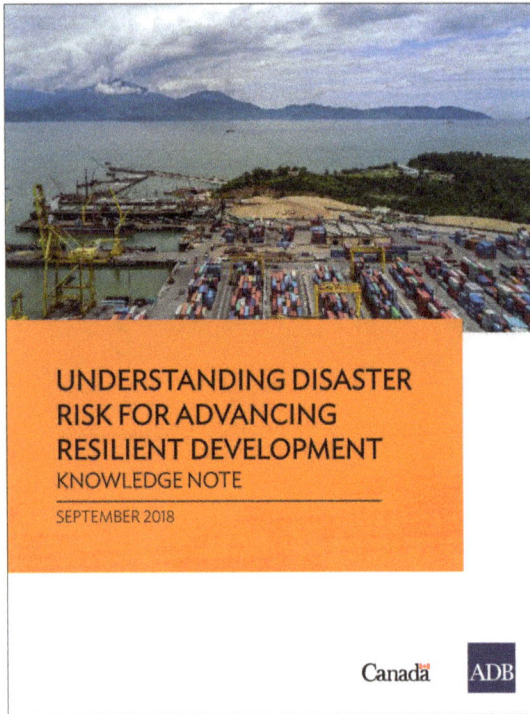

UNDERSTANDING DISASTER RISK FOR ADVANCING RESILIENT DEVELOPMENT
KNOWLEDGE NOTE

SEPTEMBER 2018

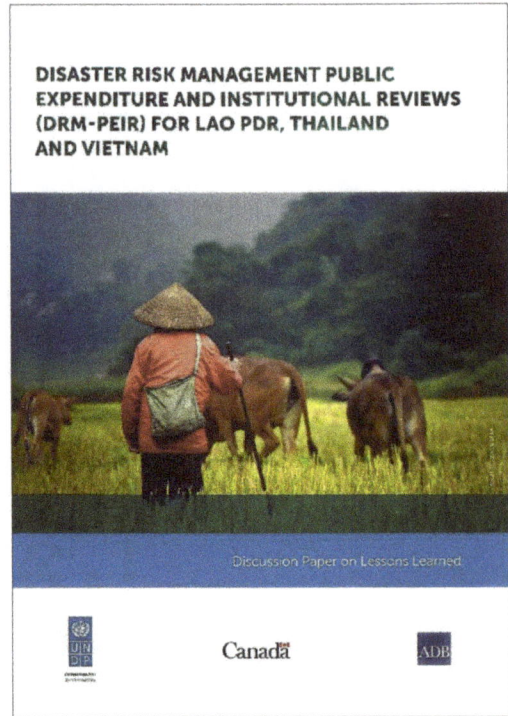

DISASTER RISK MANAGEMENT PUBLIC EXPENDITURE AND INSTITUTIONAL REVIEWS (DRM-PEIR) FOR LAO PDR, THAILAND AND VIETNAM

Discussion Paper on Lessons Learned

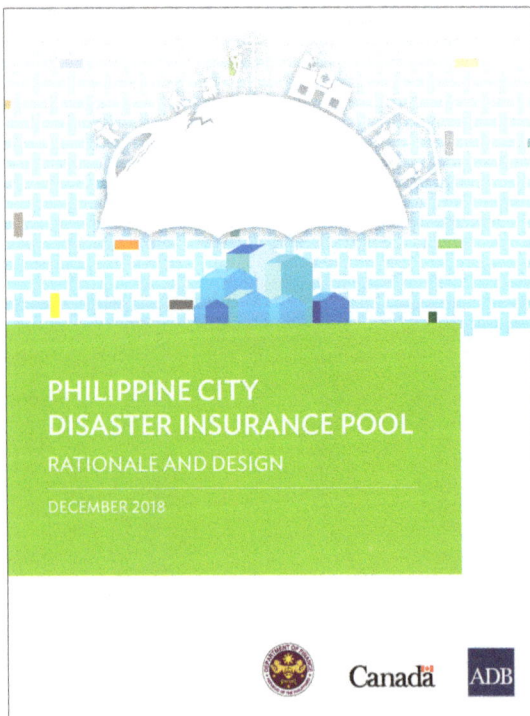

PHILIPPINE CITY DISASTER INSURANCE POOL
RATIONALE AND DESIGN

DECEMBER 2018

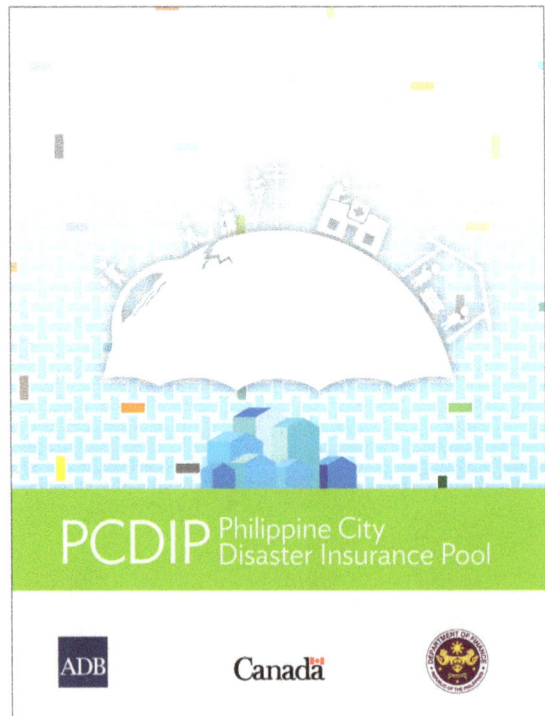

PCDIP Philippine City Disaster Insurance Pool

RISK INFORMED DEVELOPMENT
using Disaster Risk Information for Resilience

Conference Report,
27-29 August 2018, Bangkok

PUBLIC FINANCE
AND DRM EXPENDITURE
IN THAILAND

POLICY BRIEF
May 2018

FINAL REPORT
ON DISASTER RISK MANAGEMENT
PUBLIC EXPENDITURE AND
INSTITUTIONAL REVIEW (DRM-PEIR)
IN THAILAND

Fiscal Years 2012-2015

PROCEEDINGS OF THE
REGIONAL KNOWLEDGE
FORUM ON POST-DISASTER
RECOVERY

20-21 October 2015
Asian Development Bank

ASIAN DEVELOPMENT BANK

Shared Lessons on Post-Disaster Recovery

Linking Post-Disaster Recovery to Development

STRENGTHENING CITY DISASTER RISK FINANCING IN VIET NAM

ASIAN DEVELOPMENT BANK

6th ASIA-PACIFIC CLIMATE CHANGE ADAPTATION FORUM

17–19 October 2018
Manila, Philippines

Enabling Resilience for All:
Avoiding the Worst Impacts

SUMMARY REPORT

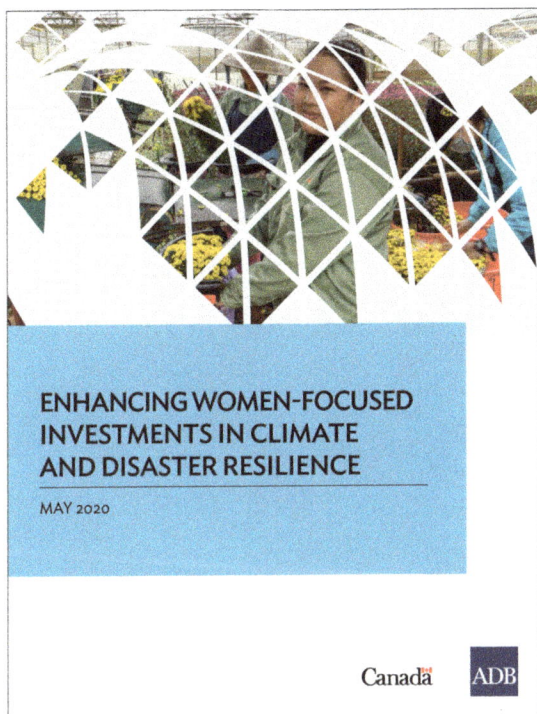

ENHANCING WOMEN-FOCUSED INVESTMENTS IN CLIMATE AND DISASTER RESILIENCE

MAY 2020

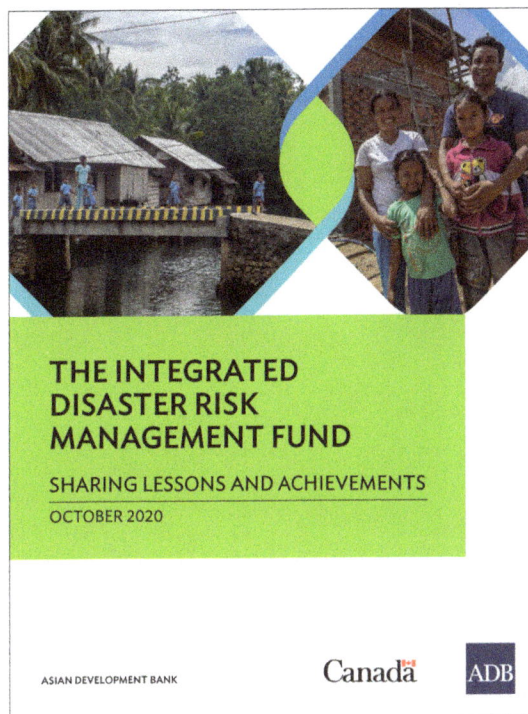

THE INTEGRATED DISASTER RISK MANAGEMENT FUND

SHARING LESSONS AND ACHIEVEMENTS

OCTOBER 2020

ASIAN DEVELOPMENT BANK

Integrated Disaster Risk Management Fund

Building resilience against disaster through an integrated disaster risk management (IDRM) approach

Natural hazards continue to cause significant loss of life in Asia and the Pacific. Direct physical losses from the disasters are not only following a steady upward path, but are also rising more rapidly than the regional gross domestic product. However, rising disaster losses are **not inevitable** and can be reduced by **investing in disaster resilience**.

Asian Development Bank's Integrated Disaster Risk Management (IDRM) approach brings together

Disaster risk reduction (DRR): Investments to enhance hazard management, including risk assessment and measures to reduce exposure and vulnerability

Climate change adaptation (CCA): Planning for changes in the intensity and frequency of natural hazards and taking actions to reduce risk both today and many years into the future

Disaster risk financing (DRF): Development and application of financing strategies to manage and transfer residual risk, including through the use of insurance and capital market instruments

The Integrated Disaster Risk Management (IDRM) Fund was established by the Asian Development Bank (ADB) in 2013, with support from the Government of Canada, as a resource to assist the development of **regional IDRM solutions** in line with the disaster risk management priorities of ADB's developing member countries (DMCs) in **Southeast Asia**, i.e., **Cambodia, Indonesia, Lao People's Democratic Republic, Myanmar, Philippines, Thailand**, and **Viet Nam**. The IDRM Fund will support activities that reflect regional applications and opportunities for cross-border benefits for disaster risk management.

SCOPE OF THE IDRM FUND

Risk Identification and Analysis: Risk Information Infrastructure, aggregation or risk data, risk profiling

Disaster Risk Reduction and Climate Change Adaption: Urban risk reduction, development of incentives for IDRM, strengthening of fiscal and legislative support for IDRM

Disaster Risk Financing: Design of disaster risk financing solutions, development of public–private partnership models for DRF

Community-based and Gender-focused IDRM: Peer-to-peer learning among grassroots organizations, investments in transboundary community-based DRM

Regional Cooperation in IDRM: Support for ongoing regional IDRM initiatives

Knowledge and Tools: Awareness raising, capacity building of policy makers

Eligibility criteria for accessing the IDRM Fund

- DMC agencies in Southeast Asia, development partners, regional and subregional institutions, and relevant regional departments of ADB are eligible for IDRM Fund resources.
- Regional projects that can be implemented in three or more of ADB's DMCs in Southeast Asia and that have an implementation period of less than 3 years.
- Projects consistent with regional disaster risk management priorities of Southeast Asia DMCs, with the objectives of ADB's country partnership strategy and results framework in each participating country, and with the objectives of ADB's Disaster and Emergency Assistance Policy.
- Projects that introduce innovative solutions in establishing proactive and scaled-up approaches to IDRM, and that are linked to ongoing regional disaster risk management programs endorsed by DMCs.
- Projects that support strong engagement with civil society and the private sector, and that enhance gender equality and social inclusion.
- Projects that support strong engagement with civil society and the private sector, and that enhance gender equality and social inclusion.

About the Asian Development Bank

ADB's vision is an Asia and Pacific region free of poverty. Its mission is to help its developing member countries reduce poverty and improve the quality of life of their people. Despite the region's many successes, it remains home to the majority of the world's poor. ADB is committed to reducing poverty through inclusive economic growth, environmentally sustainable growth, and regional integration.

Based in Manila, ADB is owned by 67 members, including 48 from the region. Its main instruments for helping its developing member countries are policy dialogue, loans, equity investments, guarantees, grants, and technical assistance.

About the Government of Canada

The Government of Canada's Southeast Asia Regional Program aims to reduce poverty in the region by facilitating economic growth and improving human rights. The program aims to strengthen regional institutions, organizations, and processes to address transboundary issues such as disaster risk and hazards that can have an impact on multiple countries.

In many countries, disasters can severely compromise hard-won development gains and divert needed resources to costly reconstruction efforts. Reducing economic and human vulnerability to disasters is one way to ensure steady economic growth in regions that are vulnerable to natural hazards.

This program is undertaken with the financial support of the Government of Canada provided through Global Affairs Canada.

For more information on how to access the Fund, visit www.adb.org/themes/environment/disaster-risk-management

© Asian Development Bank. Publication Stock No. ARM135793-3 November 2015

Printed on recycled paper

Source: ADB. Funds and Resources. *Integrated Disaster Risk Management Fund.* www.adb.org/what-we-do/funds/integrated-disaster-risk-management-fund.

Integrated Disaster Risk Management Fund

Call for Proposals-2

Small grant projects on Community-based Disaster Risk Management

Deadline to submit proposals: 31 January 2016

ADB's Integrated Disaster Risk Management Fund (IDRM Fund) for Southeast Asia supported by the Government of Canada invites proposals to implement small grant projects for **community-based disaster risk management (DRM)** in Southeast Asian developing member countries (DMCs) of ADB – Cambodia, Indonesia, Lao People's Democratic Republic, Myanmar, the Philippines, Thailand, and Viet Nam.

This call for proposals -2 will finance small grant projects under a regional technical assistance project supported by the IDRM Fund and will be implemented in close coordination with other activities of the technical assistance. The call for proposal-1 was issued in January 2014 and is currently supporting four small grant projects focusing on integration of DRM in local development planning processes; development of innovative financial products to enhance residual risk management at community level; and strengthening the role of women in disaster resilience. *For more information on the regional technical assistance, visit: http://www.adb.org/projects/47228-001/main.*

Who can submit project proposals?

- Local governments of Southeast Asian DMCs
- Civil society organizations (CSOs) which include nongovernment organizations (NGOs), networks of organizations, professional associations, foundations, independent research institutes, community-based organizations, faith-based organizations, people's organizations, youth groups, social movements, and labor unions who are registered to operate in the country where the project will be implemented. CSOs selected for funding will have to provide proof of such legal status.
- Proposals from local CSOs working closely with local governments will be preferred. International NGOs are also eligible to apply, provided the proposal demonstrates that their local counterparts will take the lead in implementation.

What are the project requirements?

- **Participation** of local governments and civil society including target communities in identifying disaster and climate risks, prioritizing needs; supporting implementation of **non-structural** interventions; and helping implementation of prioritized **structural** interventions by linking with investments of local governments and/or development partners;
- Address the underlying causes of vulnerability as identified by target community, and recognize **women as agents of change** for strengthening disaster resilience
- Demonstrate **innovation** in strengthening disaster resilience at the community level or focus on elements to strengthen the enabling environment for **scaling up** community-based DRM interventions through regular development processes;
- Benefitting **ongoing or planned projects of government and/or ADB** that focus on DRM or wider community-driven development
- Addressing community-level DRM **issues common in Southeast Asian DMCs** through **single country interventions**, with **lessons that can be shared regionally**.
- Cost not more than **US$75,000**; and
- Have an implementation period of **12 months**.

What are the priority topics?

- Strengthening **linkages between DRM and climate change adaptation** at the community level
- Strengthening community **disaster resilience in urban areas**

Submission guidelines

- Proposals should be submitted by **31 January 2016**. Proposals will be subject to review and revision, and ADB reserves the right not to select any of the proposals.
- Proposals should be submitted using the attached application form.
- Proposals should be sent by e-mail to idrm@adb.org, by fax to +632-636-2193, or by post to #6 ADB Avenue, Mandaluyong City 1550, Metro Manila, Philippines

For more information on the IDRM Fund, visit http://www.adb.org/site/funds/funds/integrated-disaster-risk-management-fund

Source: ADB. Funds and Resources. *Integrated Disaster Risk Management Fund.* www.adb.org/what-we-do/funds/integrated-disaster-risk-management-fund.

www.ingramcontent.com/pod-product-compliance
Lightning Source LLC
Chambersburg PA
CBHW061225270326
41927CB00025B/3497